Dinner

Dinner

*120 Vegan and Vegetarian Recipes for the
Most Important Meal of the Day*

Meera Sodha

FLATIRON
BOOKS
NEW YORK

Contents

Eat the seasons

Alternative contents

Introduction

A couple of years ago, I lost my love for food.

I didn't want to shop. I didn't want to cook. I ate for necessity, not pleasure.

It wasn't just food; everything around me had transformed into shades of monochrome. I couldn't get out of bed most days and I didn't care much for whether the day turned to night. I'd love to tell you that there was a single neat reason for why this happened but, like life, the truth is messy.

This loss left me feeling empty. Food was how I spent my days and paid my bills. It was the language I spoke fluently. Food was how I navigated my emotions and memory and how I tapped into my past, bringing to life my family history that had existed in countries beyond England, in India and Africa and before I was born.

I willed the emptiness to go away but it refused to budge. It went on for weeks and then months. All I knew was that I wanted and needed to find a way back and fast, for myself and the people around me.

Then one day, Hugh, my husband, who had been keeping our two young daughters and me afloat (and fed) while somehow doing his own high-pressure job, admitted that he was starting to crack under the weight of it all. When I saw the person I love struggle, something shifted in me and, like a knee-jerk reaction, I stepped back into the kitchen, grabbed a pan and began to cook again.

I wanted nothing more than for him to be okay, and the only way I really knew how to communicate that was by cooking for him. I made him dinner that night, nothing fancy, but something he loved; it was a simple Malaysian dal, similar to one that we had both eaten in the hawker markets in Singapore.

After a decade when food had been my job, cooking this meal for Hugh felt completely different. For years, I had been locked into a relentless pursuit of new dishes and new ideas, and this had taken over everything. I'd disappear for hours into cookbooks and magazines,

researching potential recipes, testing five variations of a new idea in search of the perfect dish. I'd cook for work but rarely for my family or friends. I'd completely lost sight of what food is for – but in that moment with Hugh, I found it again.

While we ate, neither of us talked about how this could be the start of a path out of my darkness, or how his admission might have given me back the keys to the kitchen. Instead, we ate happily and hungrily.

The next day, I started to cook again with one new rule: I would cook for pleasure, not work. I wanted to try to become more aware of my mood and feelings and work out what I wanted to eat, and slowly but surely, like kindling catching, I started to feel the fire in my belly again.

If the food was particularly good, I'd record it in an old orange notebook, and next to each recipe I'd write the date and what had happened that day. The old orange book filled up fast, and as it did, I realized I was drawn to one meal above the others: dinner.

Unlike breakfast, which was usually toast at the kitchen counter, or lunch, straitjacketed within the working day, our evening meal – our dinner – became the most important meal of our family life.

I found that just thinking about it and planning it had the power to ground me and pick me up after a bad day. If Hugh, the girls and I had been apart all day, dinner was a chance for us to come together again. If it was a really good day, dinner became a chance to reflect and celebrate this. Dinner felt like a response button I could push, something that I felt entirely in control of – when so much had felt out of my control.

The more I spoke to friends and family about dinner, the more I realized that others felt the same way about its power. Set against the pace of modern life, some enjoyed the meditative process of preparing a meal, while others liked the chance to explore and get creative. Some just saw it as a time to reclaim the day for themselves. Whatever they cooked, it was hardly ever fancy or remotely close to what social media tells you other people are cooking.

The recipes in this book are deeply personal. That's because they are the recipes from my orange book. They are the answers to the question I asked myself each day – what's for dinner? – when I was choosing to focus on myself again. They are the recipes that have in part (alongside a lot of therapy and support) given me back a sense of myself, and are what I really love to cook in the kitchen.

They are the dishes I eat most often with the people I love the most. Some you will recognize from my New Vegan column in the *Guardian*, but many you won't. All of them are vegan or vegetarian, as that is still, in the main, how I love to eat.

Many have been inspired by some incredible post-pandemic trips to Thailand and Taiwan and all have been led by the rumblings of my tummy, the ingredients in my pantry or meals I've eaten in homes or restaurants here or abroad. These recipes are simply a collection of where my heart has taken me.

This wasn't the book I had thought I'd write next, but following a difficult personal time and much reflection, it became the book I felt I must write. The ability to put a good dinner on the table has become my superpower. I believe it's a potent tool we all possess to make a positive change to our days, to our relationships and to our lives, and so I want it to become your superpower too, every night of the week.

The orange book that started all this is now dog-eared, covered in splatters of sauce and packed with recipes. As I write this, my daughters are still young and mostly eating tomato pasta, but one day that book will be one of the greatest things I can give them.

After all, when we can cook a good dinner each night, we have one of the most important ingredients for a life well-lived – and no one can take that away from us.

A note on . . .

How this book works

I've organized this book by categories of ingredients such as vegetable types or pulses because that is often my starting point when I'm thinking about dinner, and perhaps yours too. A little jar of kimchi in the fridge might catch my eye, or a big bowl of ripe, juicy tomatoes sat brazenly on the side will prove too much to resist, or the autumnal weather will usher me toward things I can easily roast, like squashes and celery root. Or I might need to use up a head of broccoli (as I do on a weekly basis). But it always starts with one ingredient.

Then I'll ask myself the same thing: what do I want to eat? The result is a type of meal: a curry, a dal, some noodles, a roast of sorts, salad or rice, suggestions for which can be found in the alternative contents on pp 6–7 alongside seasonal offerings.

Although 100 of the recipes in this book are dedicated to the evening meal, because, with less time and energy on my side, that is where I like to focus my efforts, there are some suggestions for starters on p 15 (mostly things that can be bought in supermarkets or food involving the lightest bit of cooking). I have also indicated which recipes could be easily served (in smaller portions) as starters.

In this chapter "Side show" on p 259 I have included ten sides. Some, like the cooked greens and the simple salads, were designed with flexibility in mind, i.e., dishes that would taste delicious with most things. Others, like the asparagus thoran or Thai salad, can also be thought of as centerpieces that would be almost aggrieved to be called a "side."

The most important chapter is, of course, "Happy endings" (p 283), in which there are ten recipes for desserts. They range from a quick way to elevate store-bought ice cream (bubble tea ice cream), a shortcut to making the legendary Thai rotis (spoiler: it's phyllo), to a vegan cheesecake that took me months to perfect.

And finally, in "Extra helpings" (p 304), there are some recipes for a few extras that I consider vital to the dinner game, such as foolproof rice, chapattis and naans, as well as little pickles that bring a bit of extra razzle-dazzle to proceedings.

Portion sizes

There are lots of variables when it comes to portion sizes, not least people's appetites and what else is being served alongside, so take this as a rule of thumb:

Rice: 3 oz dry rice per person.
Lentils: 3 oz dried lentils per person (unless lentils are the main ingredient, then up to 3½ oz) or half a can of cooked pulses.
Noodles or pasta: 3 to 3½ oz per person.
Vegetables: 10 oz raw vegetables per person.
Tofu, paneer and eggs: 4½ oz per person or 2 eggs.

Ingredients

Onions, shallots, garlic and ginger: Peel before using, unless otherwise specified.

Salt: Fine sea salt, unless otherwise specified.

Milk: Always whole, whether coconut, dairy or oat.

Cooking oil: Any neutral oil can be used in these recipes. I like to use a good-quality cold-pressed canola oil for multiple reasons. It has a high smoke point, so I can fry with it, but due to the quality I can also use it in salad dressings. It's high in monounsaturated fats, much like olive oil, and low in saturated fats.

Flours: When measuring, gently spoon flours into the measuring cup and level off with the back of a knife.

Dinner accompaniments

Where there's a suggested accompaniment to a meal, like rice or bread, I'd recommend you make the rice in advance if it's a quick meal, because when covered it will remain hot for an hour. If you're warming naan or other breads, it's best to heat them just before eating. Heat them in the microwave, two at a time, for 30 seconds, turn and heat for another 30 seconds or until hot, then keep warm under a kitchen towel or wrapped in foil until serving.

Recipe timings

The "prep" time is an estimate of how long it takes to prepare the items in the ingredients list, assuming they are in front of you, e.g., to peel and chop potatoes. The "cook" or "assemble" time is an estimate of how long the method takes to complete (whether hands-on or hands-off), such as boiling the potatoes then mashing them.

Equipment

A sharp knife, digital scales and a set of good measuring spoons will take you far. A garlic press, a large ovenproof saucepan and an 11-inch sauté pan for which you have lids, a couple of large baking sheets (I like the 16- x 12-inch size) and a reusable baking mat will take you nearly all the way. For the final mile, and because we're in the business of processing vegetables, a blender (I use a Nutribullet in this book) and a food processor will help you to complete the journey to the magical land of dinner faster and with more efficiency.

Adapting recipes for young children

If you're cooking for young children, feel free to drop the chilli in any of these recipes (I do), lower the salt (you can always add more to your portion at the table) and add strong spices like black pepper, cumin or cardamom a quarter teaspoon at a time until they taste right to you.

Key

V or VO: vegan or vegan option.

DF or DFO: dairy-free or dairy-free option.

GF or GFO: gluten-free or gluten-free option.

Many of the recipes in this book are gluten-free bar one ingredient: soy sauce, because it is often made by fermenting soybeans with wheat. To make these recipes gluten-free, use a tamari-style soy sauce instead.

To start with

Given that you're here now, I'm assuming we've tacitly agreed that dinner is where all your energy should be directed. But that's not to say that you shouldn't include an appetite-whetting nibble or some starters if you're having friends around to stretch things out. I'm not an animal.

I say "having friends around" rather than "having a dinner party" because the latter is still being held in a chokehold by the 1980s, from where it casts a dark shadow of fear on anyone wanting to invite friends over for dinner. It did, until recently, on me.

Until a few years ago, I was guilty of royally kippering myself before people came over. I'd polish the house like a dental hygienist, get dolled up as if I were going out, then I'd make multiple courses that I'd still be cooking in a sweaty puddle while my friends all had a happy time at the dinner table. It wasn't fun, and I suspected I was doing it all wrong. Then, one day, I saw the light.

Our friends, the Adamos, invited us for dinner. Ben had made dinner in advance (dan dan noodles), so we all talked and drank cocktails until tummies started to rumble and Ben popped into the kitchen to bring us a bite to eat.

Miraculously, he came back three minutes later with a small pyramid of hot takoyaki balls covered in takoyaki sauce, mayonnaise and blush-pink bonito flakes that were waving at us in the heat. He handed around napkins and forks and we all dug in. It had everything: fun, flair, flavor! No one cared that he'd microwaved them from frozen. They were delicious and we were happy to have him back into the fold so quickly. I realized this: the bar will always feel high if you're the host, but people (in general) will just be grateful to be looked after.

Now, I'm not suggesting you microwave all your starters, but I am going to suggest that you get to know your supermarket shelves and those of your local Chinese, Indian or Korean supermarket if you're lucky enough to have one nearby (there's a list of suppliers on p 310 if not). Rummaging around in the freezer has become one of my greatest pleasures, second to actually spending proper time with good friends around the table.

Low effort, high reward

This is my favorite way to prepare a snack or starter — where very little needs to be done except for a spot of boiling or blending, or bunging something in the oven, or pan-frying at most.

Chips and dips: I never met a human who didn't love chips. Either buy the best salted chips you can or the most tempting chips from your nearest East Asian supermarket. There's a galaxy of flavors out there, from spicy tomato to sweet potato and even seaweed. Salted egg yolk is my favorite. You could also place good-quality salted chips in a shallow-lipped bowl, criss-cross with some Kewpie mayonnaise and add finely sliced red, or pickled red, chillies or furikake — a delicious pre-bought mixture of seaweed, sesame seeds, sugar and salt.

Boiled broccolini and sesame sauce: Broccolini is a perfectly formed finger food to swipe through dips. Boil around three stems per person for 5 to 6 minutes, drain well and serve with the sesame dipping sauce on p 309.

Frozen dumplings and scallion pancakes: These dumplings are one of the greatest gifts to the dinner game. They can be boiled, steamed or fried to perfection. With a dipping sauce (p 233), you're in seventh heaven. The pancakes, pan-fried and sliced, make great nibbles when served with a sesame dipping sauce (p 309).

Frozen aloo parathas and samosas can be found in Indian supermarkets. Fry the paratha, slice up and serve with lime pickle yogurt (p 140). Bake the samosas and serve with cilantro chutney (p 308).

High(er) effort, high reward

If you're keen on making something more elaborate, I don't blame you. Often the line between a starter and a main course is portion size, and there is a plethora of things in this book that could be repurposed for a smaller bite:

Cheddar and gochujang cornbread (p 107) cut into thin slices; place the pickled corn salad on top at the last minute and serve with a little crème fraîche spiked with lime.

Sweet potato summer rolls (p 175), a perfect make-ahead starter.

Borlotti beans, chopped salad and tahini (p 155), served with warmed sliced flatbread for scooping.

Turnip cake (p 272) is an excellent starter. It can be made in advance, but the slices will need frying just before serving.

Kimchi and tofu dumplings (p 233) can be made ahead and kept in a sealed food container in layers separated by parchment paper, so they don't stick — until you need to fry them.

Rojak salad with avocado, tofu and tamarind (p 76) is a perfect preamble to the Malaysian dal (p 160), the 18-carat laksa (p 172) or the chickpea and potato curry (p 190). Slice the avocado and apple at the last minute (lest they brown) and toss just before serving.

Eggplants

Eggplants roasted in satay sauce

I don't look for dependability or empathy in a friend; I look for them to have at least one or ideally two fridge shelves dedicated to condiments, pickles and sauces. Among the top tier of sauces is Indonesian satay sauce, because it is the embodiment of joy and life. In fact, this sauce is also trustworthy and highly respectful of whatever it comes into contact with – perhaps it is, in fact, the perfect friend?

SERVES 4

3 large eggplants (2½ lbs)
canola oil
salt
7 large shallots (8½ oz net), *halved and thinly sliced*
2 cloves of garlic, *crushed*
2 long red chillies, *finely chopped*
2 sticks of lemongrass, *outer leaves and top third discarded, the rest finely chopped*
¾ x ¾ inch ginger, *grated*
1 tbsp dark soy sauce
1 tbsp tamarind paste
1½ tsp soft light brown sugar
1 cup crunchy peanut butter

to serve
a handful of fresh mint, cilantro and dill leaves, *chopped*
a handful of store-bought crispy fried onions
cooked jasmine rice *(p 304)*

Preheat the oven to 425°F and line a roasting pan with parchment paper.

Cut each eggplant into an eggplant "octopus": keeping the green top of the eggplant intact, slice down lengthways through the middle, then turn it 90 degrees and slice down lengthways again, to create four "legs." Slice down each leg in half, to create eight legs.

Arrange the eggplants head to foot on the tray, drizzle over 2 tablespoons of oil and rub it into all the nooks and crannies. Do the same with a little salt, both inside and outside, then roast for 30 minutes until soft.

While the eggplants are roasting, make the sauce. Heat ¼ cup of oil in a frying pan over a medium to low heat and, once it's hot, add the shallots, garlic, chillies, lemongrass and ginger, and fry, stirring regularly, for 15 to 20 minutes, until soft and translucent. Stir in the soy sauce, tamarind paste, sugar, ¾ teaspoon of salt and the peanut butter, and cook, stirring, for a couple of minutes. Slowly pour in 1⅔ cups of water, mixing it in as you go, to create a thick sauce, then take off the heat.

Once the eggplants have had their roasting time, pour the sauce all over them, making sure some of it goes inside all the cuts, then pop back in the oven for 10 minutes.

To serve, scatter over the herbs and fried onions. Serve with freshly steamed jasmine rice, and a salad if you like.

V   PREP 15 mins / COOK 1 hr 10mins

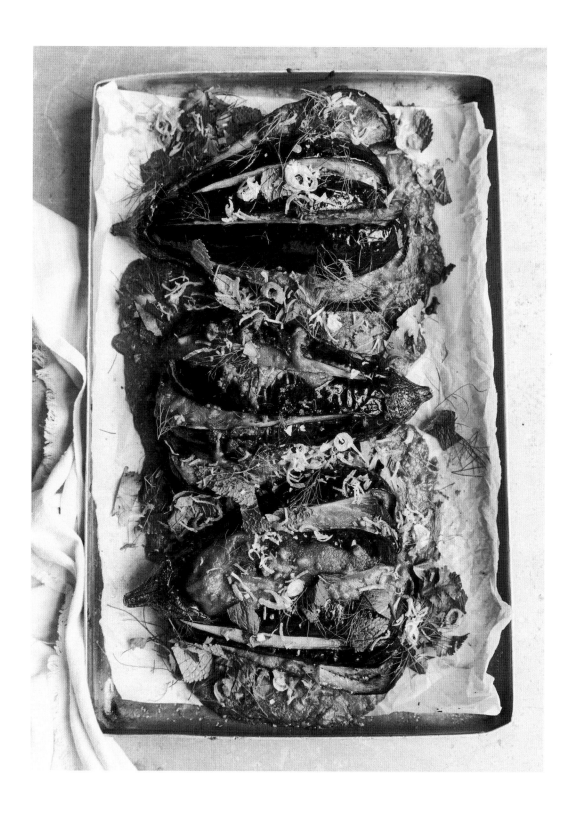

Eggplant, green bean and tofu pad kra pao

Pad kra pao, which translates as "holy basil stir-fry," is a contender for the most popular and beloved street-food dish of Thailand. I like to call it "kraPOW!" because its starring ingredient, holy basil, has a very vibrant clove-meets-pepper flavor that, tossed through at the last minute, gives whopping great strength, beauty and vitality to this dish.

NOTE Kecap manis is a sweet, spice-infused soy-based sauce and, like holy basil, can be found in East Asian supermarkets. If you can't find holy basil, substitute it with Thai basil.

SERVES 4

2 large eggplants (1½ lbs), *cut into 1-inch cubes*

canola oil

salt

10½ oz fine green beans, *tailed*

10 oz extra-firm tofu, *drained*

7 large shallots (8½ oz net), *finely sliced*

¾ × ¾ inch ginger, *grated*

7 cloves of garlic, *crushed*

3 bird's-eye chillies, *finely chopped*

1½ tbsp rice vinegar

3 tbsp kecap manis

3 tbsp dark soy sauce

1½ tbsp toasted sesame oil

¾ oz fresh holy or Thai basil, *leaves picked and torn*

1 lime, *halved*

to serve

optional: 1 bird's-eye chilli, *finely sliced*

cooked jasmine rice *(p 304)*

Preheat the oven to 425°F.

Tip the eggplant onto a large baking sheet (or two) lined with parchment paper – make sure the cubes have plenty of room – drizzle with ¼ cup of oil, scatter over a teaspoon of salt, mix, then roast for 30 minutes. Put the beans on top, stir so that the beans are coated in the oil and roast for another 10 minutes, until all the vegetables are tender.

Pat the tofu dry with paper towel and cut into ½-inch cubes. Heat 2 tablespoons of oil in a wide nonstick frying pan and fry the tofu until crispy and brown all over, then transfer to a plate.

Heat 2 more tablespoons of oil in the same pan, then add the shallots, ginger, garlic and chillies and fry, stirring, for 10 minutes, until the shallots are nice and soft. Add the vinegar, kecap manis, soy sauce and sesame oil, stir everything together and cook for 2 minutes. Take off the heat and stir in the roasted vegetables, fried tofu and half the basil.

Squeeze over the lime, scatter with the remaining basil, add a little extra sliced chilli if you wish and serve with jasmine rice.

Shandong's treasures

Thanks to ancient trade routes, many countries have eggplants, potatoes and peppers in their vegetable drawers. In India they're invariably curried, while in Greece they form a roast called *briami*. However, in Shandong in Northern China the vegetables are fried until soft, then tossed with heady, sweet Shaoxing wine and soy sauce to create a light, fresh but rich stir-fry called Di San Xian, meaning "the three treasures of the earth." Shandong wins this round.

NOTE   This is a quick recipe, so make the rice first if you're eating it alongside.

SERVES 4

1½ tbsp cornstarch
canola oil
2 large waxy potatoes (1 lb),
   peeled and cut into wedges
   1 inch at the widest point
2 eggplants (1 lb), *cut into*
   1½- × ¾-inch lozenges
2 green bell peppers (12 oz), *cut*
   into irregular 1- × 1½-inch pieces
4 cloves of garlic, *finely sliced*
1 tsp salt
2 tbsp light soy sauce
2 tbsp Shaoxing wine
1 tsp ground black pepper
cooked jasmine rice *(p 304),*
   to serve

In a small bowl, mix the cornstarch with 7 tablespoons of water and set aside. Keep a very large plate nearby to transfer the cooked vegetables onto.

In a large nonstick pan for which you have a lid, heat 2 tablespoons of oil over a medium heat and, when hot, add the potatoes. Cook for 8 to 10 minutes, tossing occasionally, until brown and tender (they shouldn't resist a knife when prodded). Using a slotted spoon, remove the potatoes and put them on the prepared plate.

Add another tablespoon of oil to the pan, then add the eggplants. Cook for 3 minutes on each side until brown, then put the lid on for a couple of minutes. Remove the lid and check the eggplants: they should be very soft. Tip the eggplants onto the same plate as the potatoes, then add another tablespoon of oil to the pan and, when hot, add the peppers.

Let them blister in the hot oil for about 4 minutes, until they have softened a little, then add 1 final tablespoon of oil and the sliced garlic. Stir-fry for a minute, then put the cooked vegetables back into the pan and add the salt, soy sauce, Shaoxing wine, black pepper and the cornstarch mix. Stir to coat the vegetables, adding more water if need be: you want the sauce to coat all the vegetables. Toss and simmer for a couple of minutes, then take off the heat. Serve with jasmine rice.

Eggplants

Nam jim eggplant salad with wild rice

Up and down the length and breadth of Thailand's tables, you'll find dipping sauces of various kinds waiting patiently to add fire and life to your meal. Nam jim is a particular favorite of mine, and, although there are many variations, it is always fabulously punchy when made with chillies, sugar, garlic, lime and a salty element (such as fish sauce or soy). Here, I've doused some roasted eggplants in the sauce, then tossed them with wild rice and fresh herbs to add some fire and life to your table.

NOTE You can buy pre-mixed basmati and wild rice from larger supermarkets. You'll need a pestle and mortar to make the nam jim dressing.

SERVES 4

eggplants
4 medium eggplants (2½ lbs)
canola oil
1½ cups basmati and wild rice
salt

nam jim dressing
1 oz fresh cilantro, *leaves picked, stems finely sliced*
3 cloves of garlic, *peeled*
3 bird's-eye chillies, *chopped*
1 tbsp dark brown sugar
2 tbsp light soy sauce
5 tbsp lime juice, *from 2–3 limes*
3 tbsp orange juice, *from 1 orange*
¾ oz fresh Thai basil, *leaves shredded*
¾ oz fresh mint, *leaves shredded*

Preheat the oven to 400°F. Cut the eggplant into long wedges, ¾ inch at the widest part, put into a large bowl, pour over ¼ cup of oil and toss to coat. Arrange the eggplants in a single layer across two baking sheets (keep the bowl for later) and bake for 25 minutes, turning halfway through.

While the eggplants are roasting, cook the rice. Put the rice in a sieve and rinse really well until the water runs clear. Tip into a saucepan (for which you have a tight-fitting lid), cover with 1¾ cups of cold water and ½ teaspoon of salt, put the lid on and bring to a boil. As soon as the water boils, turn the heat down to a whisper and cook for 20 minutes. After this time, turn the heat off but don't lift the lid. Allow the rice to rest while you make the dressing.

To make the dressing, put the cilantro stems, garlic, chillies and ¾ teaspoon of salt into a mortar and bash until smooth. Tip into the large bowl from earlier, and add the sugar, soy sauce, and lime and orange juices. Stir until the sugar dissolves, then add the cooked eggplants, submerge in the liquid and set aside for a few minutes.

To make up the salad, put the rice into a serving bowl, and air-lift the eggplants into the rice, leaving as much of the dressing behind as possible. Add the basil, mint and cilantro leaves to the dressing bowl, gently toss to mix, then drizzle over the top of the eggplants.

Miso eggplants with salt and vinegar kale

Eggplants and miso: what a couple. The eggplant is self-assured, tender and supportive. He's the type you can throw into any situation and he'll be great. He doesn't mind playing second fiddle to miso, who is popular, dazzling but a bit intense. She doesn't rub along well with everyone and so they're cautious about which other ingredients they let onto the plate, but make an exception for tall, dark and handsome Tuscan (lacinato) kale.

NOTE Shiro miso or sweet white miso is a smooth, pale sweet miso. Clearspring make a great and widely available one.

SERVES 4

eggplants
4 small to medium eggplants (2 lbs)
canola oil, *to brush*
3½ oz shiro or sweet white miso
¼ cup unsalted butter, *vegan or dairy, softened*
¼ cup mirin
2 cloves of garlic, *crushed*
a handful of toasted sesame seeds
(I use black and white, mixed)

Tuscan (lacinato) kale
14 oz Tuscan (lacinato) kale, *leaves stripped from stems*
2 tbsp canola oil
1 red chilli, *finely sliced*
3 tbsp white wine vinegar
2 tsp superfine sugar
1 tsp salt
¾ oz fresh mint, *leaves picked*

to serve
cooked jasmine rice *(p 304)*

Preheat the oven to 425°F.

Cut the eggplants in half lengthways, keeping the green tops on, and score the flesh with deep strokes of the knife, in a criss-cross pattern. Brush with oil and put them into the oven for 20 minutes, until the flesh is softening and starting to turn golden.

While the eggplants are baking, make up the miso butter. Put the miso, butter, mirin and garlic into a bowl and mix well. When the eggplants have had their 20 minutes in the oven, carefully spread 1½ tablespoons of paste on the face of each one, evenly coating every bit of the surface, then put them into the oven again for 15 minutes, until the miso butter is a burnished gold. Remove from the oven and scatter over the sesame seeds.

To cook the greens, heat 2 tablespoons of oil in a large frying pan for which you have a lid. When hot, add the kale and pop the lid on. Cook for 2 minutes, then remove the lid, turn the leaves and add ¼ cup of water. Pop the lid on again and cook for another 2 minutes, then turn the leaves and cook for a final 2 minutes, or until the kale is tender and burnt in places. Add the chilli, vinegar, sugar, salt and mint, then mix and take off the heat. To serve, give each person two halves of the eggplant with some greens and jasmine rice.

Baked eggplants, chickpeas and tomatoes

Give a man a frying pan, and he can stand by the stove and make himself dinner. Give a man some baking sheets, and he is free to sit on the sofa and watch Netflix while dinner cooks itself. With that in mind, I've adapted one of my favorite things to eat: a scoopable tomato, chickpea and eggplant dish – made with just enough spice to raise an eyebrow – into an oven-based recipe.

NOTE You'll need a very large baking sheet (or two medium) for the eggplants and a high-sided baking dish, 16- × 12-inches, for the tomatoes.

SERVES 4–6

eggplants

scant ½ cup extra virgin olive oil, *plus extra to brush*

3 medium eggplants (2 lbs)

6 cloves of garlic, *crushed*

3 x 14-oz cans of chopped tomatoes

1½ tsp salt

½ tsp ground black pepper

¾ tsp ground cinnamon

2 tsp Urfa biber chilli flakes

2 x 15-oz cans of chickpeas, *drained*

tahini yogurt

¾ cup plain Greek or dairy-free yogurt

2 tbsp tahini *mixed with 2 tbsp water*

scant ½ tsp salt

to serve

a handful of fresh mint leaves, *chopped*

black pepper

flatbreads *(pp 305–7)* **or cooked** jasmine rice *(p 304)*

Preheat the oven to 400°F. Line a large baking sheet (or two medium ones) with parchment paper and brush with oil.

Chop the eggplants into ½-inch-thick rounds, put these side by side on the baking sheet(s) and brush the tops with oil.

Pour the oil into the high-sided 16- × 12-inch baking dish. Add the garlic, tomatoes, salt, pepper, cinnamon and Urfa chilli, and stir to combine.

Pop the eggplant sheet(s) and tomato dish into the oven and cook for 30 minutes, until the eggplant slices are collapsing when squished together; if they're not, bake them for another 5 to 10 minutes. Scrape the eggplants into the tomato dish, add the chickpeas and mix, then bake for another 30 minutes, by which time the sauce should be oily, dark and rich.

Meanwhile, mix the yogurt, loosened tahini and salt together in a pretty serving bowl.

To serve, spoon the eggplants, tomatoes and chickpeas into bowls. Add some generous dollops of the tahini yogurt and scatter over the chopped mint. Crack over some fresh black pepper and finish with more oil (if you like), then serve with the remaining yogurt and warmed flatbreads or rice alongside.

VO/GFO   PREP 5 mins / COOK 1 hr 10 mins

Roasted eggplant with silken tofu, tahini and crispy chilli

There are times in cooking when two plus two equals ten. A roasted eggplant by itself is perfectly nice, a drizzle of tahini, a spot of wobbly silken tofu or chilli crisp are great in their own right, but when they all come together you get the culinary equivalent of fireworks.

NOTE I use Lao Gan Ma chilli crisp, which can be found in larger supermarkets or East Asian supermarkets. Serve with some greens, like the sesame and lime broccolini on p 271.

SERVES 4

canola oil

½ tsp salt

3 medium eggplants (2 lbs), *cut into 1-inch-thick disks*

10 oz silken tofu, *drained*

¾ x ¾ inch ginger, *very finely chopped*

1 tbsp light soy sauce

2 tsp white wine vinegar

6 scallions, *finely sliced*

2 tbsp chilli crisp

½ tbsp tahini

cooked jasmine or short-grain rice
(pp 304–5), to serve

Preheat the oven to 400°F and line two large baking sheets and one small with parchment paper.

Mix ¼ cup of oil and the salt in a small bowl, then brush the oil on both sides of the eggplant slices and arrange on the two large baking sheets in a single layer. Put the tofu block on the small baking sheet, then put all the baking sheets into the oven. Bake for 20 minutes, then remove the tofu baking sheet; give the eggplants another 10 to 15 minutes, until they are golden brown, then remove those too.

While the tofu and eggplants are baking, make the sauce. Put 6 tablespoons of oil into a small saucepan with the ginger, soy sauce, vinegar, scallions, chilli crisp and tahini, bring it up to a swift boil, then take off the heat.

When the tofu is just cool enough to handle, cut it into ¼-inch-thick slices. Layer the slices of eggplant and tofu in an alternating pattern on a lipped or high-sided platter. You'll have more eggplant slices than tofu, so put the extra eggplants in the center, or layer two eggplant slices for every slice of tofu for a more uniform look. Anoint with the hot scallion chilli oil and serve over rice in bowls.

Eggplants

Eggplant donburi

What I love about donburi, or Japanese rice bowls, is that they are complete meals in themselves. Although I eat dal and curry with rice all the time, they're pretty flexible in that they could be eaten with other things too: bread, or roti, even by themselves. With donburi, rice isn't the afterthought, it's the first. It means that whatever is topping the rice, like these eggplants, has to be so intensely flavored that it needs to lean on the warm blanket of white rice to provide a respite from the potency.

NOTE I've used one of my favorite toppings for the donburi: fried, salted and vinegared scallions and ginger. If you don't have time to make it, use thinly matchsticked fresh ginger or long shreds of scallions instead.

SERVES 4

eggplants
1½ cups short-grain rice
¼ cup cooking sake
¼ cup light soy sauce
2½ tbsp mirin
2 cloves of garlic, *crushed*
3 medium eggplants (2 lbs),
    cut lengthways into ½-inch slices
canola oil

**fried ginger and
onion topping**
6 tbsp canola oil
2½ x 2½ inches ginger, *sliced into
    fine matchsticks*
6 scallions, *finely chopped*
½ tsp salt
2 tsp white wine vinegar

Wash the rice in a sieve until the water runs clear, then place in a saucepan for which you have a tight-fitting lid. Cover with warm water and soak for 5 minutes, then drain, cover with 1⅔ cups of cold water, put the lid on and bring to a boil. Turn the heat down to a whisper, cook for 12 minutes, then take the pan off the heat and put to one side, still with the lid on.

Make the donburi sauce by combining the sake, soy sauce, mirin, garlic and a pinch of the matchsticked ginger from the topping ingredients.

Line a large baking sheet with some paper towel. Heat the oil for the topping in a wide frying pan over a medium heat, add the remaining ginger and scallions and cook for about 8 minutes, until soft and beginning to caramelize. Tip into a bowl, add the salt and vinegar, stir and set aside.

Place a little more oil in the frying pan if need be, then, cooking them in batches, lay in the eggplant slices side by side. Fry for 3 minutes, or until golden brown, then turn over and fry for another 3 minutes, until tender. Transfer them onto the baking sheet. Once all the eggplants have been fried, gently place them back in the pan in layers and turn the heat down. Pour over the donburi sauce and allow it to bubble for a couple of minutes until reduced and glossy, then take off the heat. (If the sauce threatens to disappear, add a little water to rehydrate – you want this a bit saucy.)

Distribute the rice between four bowls and shape into a dome by patting the edges down with the back of a spoon. Lay slices of eggplant on top, spoon over a little sauce and scatter over the ginger and scallion topping.

Ben Benton strikes again

On any given day, I want to know what my friend the cook and writer Ben Benton is eating, because it's guaranteed to be great. I've never met a more naturally talented cook who has the ability to transform the most basic ingredients into pure magic. He has many fans of his ben ben noodles (published in *East*), and here he strikes again with a braised eggplant and celery dish that he likes to make for friends when they come for dinner. It does not disappoint; elegant and simple, it's greater than the sum of its parts.

NOTE You'll need a specific type of Lao Gan Ma chilli oil to make this, called "kohlrabi, peanuts and tofu in chilli oil." If you use another type, add it a tablespoon at a time until it tastes just right to you.

SERVES 4

2 tsp Sichuan peppercorns
3 medium eggplants (2 lbs)
canola oil, *for pan-frying*
2 stalks of celery (10 oz), *cut at a steep angle into ¾-inch pieces, any leaves reserved*
1 tsp fennel seeds
2 tbsp light soy sauce
2 tbsp rice vinegar
¼ cup Lao Gan Ma kohlrabi, peanuts and tofu in chilli oil
cooked jasmine rice *(p 304), to serve*

Lightly bash the peppercorns in a mortar — or skip this step if you're happy (as I am) to encounter a feisty little crunch in the finished dish.

Cut the eggplants in half lengthways, then cut each half into four long wedges. You'll be frying them in batches, so get a plate and a pair of tongs ready to move them around.

Put 2 tablespoons of oil into a wide nonstick pan or pot for which you have a lid over a medium to high heat. When it's shimmering hot, place the wedges of eggplant in the pan — as many as will fit next to one another, one cut side down. Cook for 2 to 3 minutes, until golden, then turn them over and add another tablespoon of oil to the pan. Fry the eggplants for another 2 minutes, then transfer them to the plate. Fry the remaining eggplants, adding a little oil each time you add or turn them. Don't worry if they're not fully cooked through: they'll be braised to softness shortly.

Put 2 more tablespoons of oil into the pan over a medium heat and, when hot, add the celery and pop the lid on. Cook for 5 minutes, tossing occasionally, then stir in the Sichaun peppercorns and fennel seeds and pop the lid on again for another 5 minutes.

Put the eggplants back into the pan and add the soy sauce, vinegar and the Lao Gan Ma, then gently stir to coat everything in the sauce. Pour in 5 tablespoons of water, pop the lid on the pan, reduce the heat to low and allow the eggplants to blip away for 15 minutes to allow the flavors to mingle. Top with celery leaves if you have any, and serve with fresh, hot jasmine rice.

V   PREP 10 mins / COOK 35 mins

Eggplant kofta in tomato and spinach sauce

The eggplant is a shape-shifter. It's hard to imagine, when you cut into that white spongy flesh, the myriad of things you could create, from crispy katsu to smoky baba ganoush. In this recipe, the eggplant is transformed into kofta, or Indian meatballs for want of a better description, which are not quite "meaty," but densely textured, lovable and satisfying lumps nevertheless. Here they are nestled into their happy place, a garam masala–spiced tomato sauce.

NOTE You'll need a food processor for this recipe. Don't skimp on the time taken to cook the eggplants: they need to be dry for the kofta to hold together.

SERVES 4
(makes 16 kofta)

canola oil

1¾ lbs eggplants (approx. 3), *cut into ½-inch cubes*

6 cloves of garlic, *crushed*

1½ tsp ground cinnamon

¾ tsp ground black pepper

½ tsp ground cumin

1½ tbsp tomato paste

¾ cup unseasoned dried breadcrumbs

salt

3 cups passata

1½ tsp Kashmiri chilli powder

1 tsp garam masala

3½ oz baby spinach

naan or flatbreads *(pp 305–6), to serve*

Heat ¼ cup of oil in a large, wide nonstick pan over a medium heat. When very hot, add the eggplants and cook, stirring regularly, for 15 minutes, until soft and browning. Add half the crushed garlic, cook for 2 minutes, then add the cinnamon, black pepper, cumin, tomato paste, breadcrumbs and 1¼ teaspoons of salt. Cook for a couple of minutes, until there is no liquid left in the pan, then take off the heat and leave to cool.

When cool, blitz in a food processor and rinse out the pan. Put the mixture onto a large plate and divide in half using a butter knife. Then divide each half into eight to get sixteen pieces (about 1¼ oz each). Roll each piece into a ball, press into a patty around 1½ inches across and place on another large plate.

To cook the kofta, heat 2 tablespoons of oil in the same nonstick pan. When hot, lay in eight kofta, spacing them well apart, and leave undisturbed for a few minutes, otherwise they'll stick to the pan. When the bottom is crisp, use a fish spatula to lever them off the pan, flip and cook until crisp and burnished mahogany all over – 8 minutes in all. Transfer to a plate and repeat with the remaining eight kofta, then set aside while you make the sauce.

Put 3 tablespoons of oil into the same pan over a low to medium heat and, when hot, add the rest of the garlic and cook for around 3 minutes, until sticky and golden. Add the passata and 1 cup of water, and leave to cook for 15 minutes, until jammy and thick. Add the chilli powder, garam masala and a teaspoon of salt, cook for 5 minutes more, then add the spinach handful by handful and stir to wilt.

Turn the heat down to a whisper, pop the kofta back into the sauce and allow to warm through gently. Serve with warmed naan for dipping and scooping.

V   PREP 10 mins / COOK 1 hr 15 mins

Anaïs's tamarind eggplants

Anaïs Ca Dao is the type of friend who will come over, sniff around in your fridge and make you lunch; while eating it, she will want to talk about what's for dinner. This dish was that dinner, born out of our mutual love for the sweet-and-sour tamarind dishes of Thailand. Cooking it involves the meditative turning of eggplants until they bronze and soften, and sweating down onions until they glisten like ruby slices. It's the perfect thing to cook when you have a friend to chat to – especially when there are more meals to be discussed.

NOTE Don't skimp on the cooking times for the eggplants and onions – it's what takes this recipe from good to great.

SERVES 2

2 large eggplants (1¼ lbs)
canola oil
2 red onions, *halved and finely sliced*
1 tsp salt
4 cloves of garlic, *finely chopped*
1 tsp chilli flakes
1 tbsp soft light brown sugar
3 tbsp tamarind paste
½ tbsp light soy sauce
½ oz fresh Thai basil, *leaves picked*
cooked jasmine rice *(p 304),*
  to serve

Cut off and discard the eggplant stalks, cut the bulbs in half lengthways, then cut each half into long wedges 1½ to 2 inches at their widest part.

Put ¼ cup of oil into a wide nonstick frying pan on a medium to high heat and have a plate ready. When the oil is hot, lay in some of the eggplant wedges on one of their cut sides and in a single layer, and leave to cook for 3 minutes. Turn the eggplant wedges on to their other cut side, cook for another 3 minutes, then transfer to the plate. Add an extra tablespoon or two of oil to the pan and repeat with the remaining eggplant wedges.

In the same pan, turn down the heat to medium, add 3 tablespoons of oil and, when hot, add the onions and salt. Stirring infrequently, sweat down the onions for about 12 minutes, until browning nicely; if they at any stage threaten to stick and burn, add a little water (up to a couple of tablespoons). Stir in the garlic and cook for 3 minutes more, or until the onions are caramelized and soft.

Add the chilli flakes, sugar, tamarind paste, soy sauce and ¾ cup of water to the pan, then stir in the eggplant wedges. Turn down the heat to medium-low, simmer for 10 minutes, then turn the eggplants and simmer for another 10 minutes, or until they are tender.

Lift out the eggplant wedges one by one onto a platter, layering them up neatly. Add the Thai basil leaves to the tamarind and onion sauce left in the pan, stir until it wilts into the mixture, then pour all over the eggplants. Serve with jasmine rice.

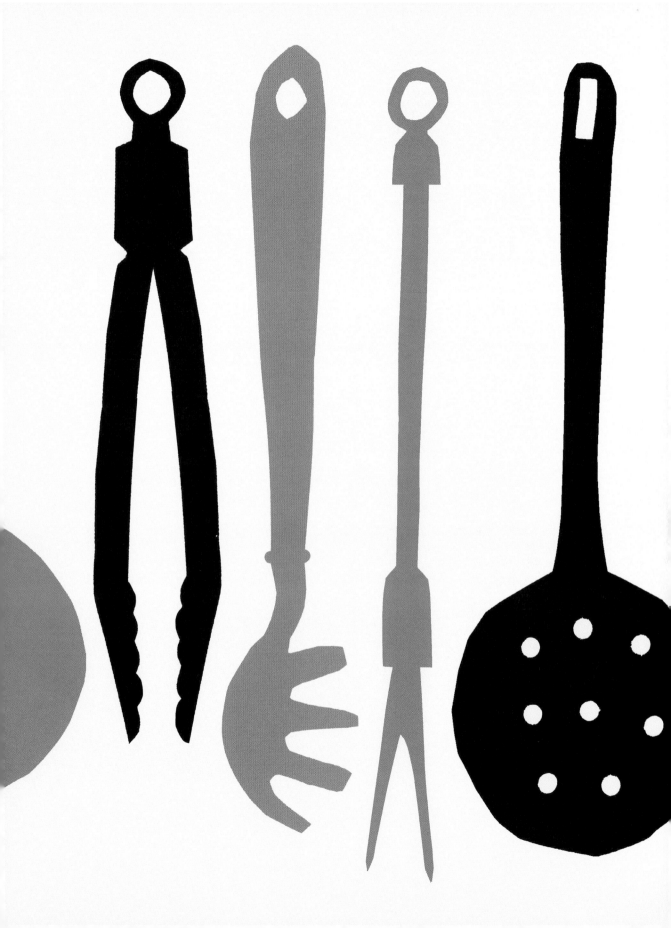

Broccoli

and

other

brassicas

Broccoli spaghetti with zhoug

The truth about broccoli is that there is always a head of it in our fridge, and so on a weekly basis I (and many other cooks, I suspect) endeavor to undertake what is known as the Great Broccoli Challenge to work out how to turn it into a meal. Here's a fine way to solve that problem. In this recipe, the broccoli and spaghetti provide a soft backdrop to zhoug, an addictive sauce popular across the Middle East. I've used fresh cilantro, jalapeños, ground cumin and cardamom, but you can treat this recipe as more of a guide than a set of rules, and use whatever herbs, chillies and spices you have on hand.

NOTE   You'll need a food processor to make this.

SERVES 4

1 head of broccoli *(12 oz or smaller)*
2 oz fresh cilantro, *roughly chopped*
1 oz fresh flat-leaf parsley, *roughly chopped*
3 jalapeño peppers, *chopped*
1½ tsp ground cumin
1½ tsp ground coriander
½ tsp ground cardamom
1½ tbsp lemon juice, *from 1 lemon*
extra virgin olive oil
salt
10 oz dried spaghetti

Chop off and discard any woody bits from the broccoli stem, then roughly chop the whole head into pieces, blitz in a food processor until super fine and scrape into a large bowl.

Next, make the zhoug. Put the fresh cilantro, parsley, jalapeños, cumin, ground coriander, cardamom, lemon juice, 5 tablespoons of oil and ½ teaspoon of salt into the food processor and blitz to a smooth paste.

Put 2 tablespoons of oil into a large nonstick frying pan over a medium heat and, when hot, add the blitzed broccoli and ½ teaspoon of salt. Cook, stirring every now and then, for about 8 minutes, until sweet and soft, then turn off the heat.

Fill a large saucepan with water, adding a teaspoon of salt per 4 cups of water. Bring to a boil and cook the spaghetti until al dente. While it's cooking, carefully dip a mug into the saucepan and collect a mugful of pasta water.

Drain the pasta and tip into the broccoli pan (or transfer the pasta into the pan using tongs), then add the zhoug and toss to combine. Pour in some of the reserved pasta cooking water to loosen it – I use 8 to 10 tablespoons – until it looks nice and saucy. Check for seasoning, adding more salt, chilli or lemon as you wish, then serve on plates or in bowls and eat while hot.

Broccoli and other brassicas

Tofu fried rice with kale

Not so much a recipe but a carnival of flavors available to you when you have some leftover rice and less than enthusiastic-looking vegetables in the fridge. My personal preference is for silken tofu and leafy greens. The tofu breaks up into creamy curds, adding body and texture, every hairdresser's dream, while the kale is sweet and juicy from greedily collecting the seasoning in its craggy emerald leaves.

NOTE Leftover rice works perfectly for fried rice because it's firmer and drier than freshly cooked. If you have some pre-cooked rice, use 4 cups in this recipe instead of cooking it from scratch, then season to taste at the end.

SERVES 4

1½ cups raw jasmine rice, or 4 cups cooked white rice
1¾ cups vegetable stock
3 tbsp canola oil
1 large yellow onion, halved and finely sliced
3 cloves of garlic, crushed
14 oz Tuscan (lacinato) kale, leaves stripped and shredded
1 tsp Chinese five-spice powder
½ tsp salt
1 tbsp toasted sesame oil
2 tbsp light soy sauce
12 oz silken tofu, drained
sriracha sauce, to serve

To cook the rice, place it in a sieve and rinse with plenty of cold water, then drain. Tip the rice into a lidded saucepan, add 1¾ cups of hot stock and bring to a boil. Place the lid on, turn the heat down to a whisper and cook for 15 minutes, then take off the heat and leave to steam with the lid on for a further 5 to 10 minutes. Remove the lid, tip out onto a large baking sheet and allow to cool.

In the meantime, put the oil into a large frying pan over a medium heat. When hot, add the onion and fry for around 8 minutes, until softened and browning. Add the garlic and cook for 2 minutes, then add the kale. Cook for 5 to 7 minutes, stirring every now and then, until wilted, then add the five-spice powder, salt, sesame oil and soy sauce. Stir, then crumble the tofu through clean fingers into the pan.

Cook for a few minutes until all the ingredients are well mixed, then add the rice. I like to use a spaghetti spoon to do this so as not to break up the rice too much. Fry until the rice is hot, mixing gently until all the ingredients are well acquainted. Check for seasoning: you may need to use extra salt if you are using pre-cooked rice, so adjust if need be. Serve in bowls and drizzle with sriracha.

Soba noodle soup with caramelized cabbage and pickles

This soup is based on the Japanese toshikoshi soba soup, or "year-crossing noodle." Traditionally, it's eaten on New Year's Eve to reflect on the past year and welcome the new one: the idea is to enjoy a long, peaceful life with each lengthy slurp and break free from the hardship of the past as the noodle breaks with each bite. In its simplest form it is made using buckwheat soba noodles and a hot dashi broth, but I've taken liberties and bolstered it with caramelized cabbage and turnip pickles.

NOTE Kombu is dehydrated seaweed and it makes a fantastic stock. You can find it in East Asian supermarkets and online (p 310). Any leftover pickled turnip can be kept in the fridge for two weeks.

SERVES 4

caramelized cabbage

2 tbsp canola oil

1 large red cabbage (1¾ lbs), *cored and chopped into ½-inch pieces*

1 red onion, *finely chopped*

¼ cup mirin

1 tbsp rice vinegar

1 tsp salt

turnip pickle

¾ tsp salt

½ cup rice vinegar

2 small turnips (7 oz), *peeled and cut into thick matchsticks*

soba noodle soup

1 large piece of kombu (*around 16 x 12 inches*)

¼ cup brown rice miso

¼ cup light soy sauce

¼ cup mirin

7 oz soba noodles

2 tbsp toasted sesame oil

2 oz watercress, *tough ends removed*

Start with the cabbage. Place a large frying pan on a medium heat, add the oil, and, when hot, add the cabbage and onion, and cook, stirring occasionally to stop it sticking, for 30 minutes. Add the mirin, vinegar and salt, and cook for 20 minutes more, by which time the cabbage should be caramelized and very tender.

While the cabbage is cooking, pickle the turnips. In a pitcher, mix the salt into the vinegar and ½ cup of freshly boiled water, then pour over the turnips in a heatproof bowl and set aside.

To make the soup, bring 6 cups of water to a boil in a medium-sized saucepan, lower the heat to a whisper, add the kombu and simmer for 10 minutes, then take off the heat. Carefully remove the kombu with a pair of tongs and discard. Whisk the miso, soy sauce and mirin into the hot broth and leave to one side.

Cook the noodles according to the package instructions, taking a minute off the cooking time, then drain and rinse under cold water. Transfer to a bowl and mix with the sesame oil.

To assemble, divide the noodles between four bowls. Gently heat up the broth, pour it over the noodles, then top with the caramelized cabbage, watercress and pickled turnips, and serve.

Whole roast cauliflower pilaf with almonds and pistachios

An excellent centerpiece. The pilaf is stuffed full of nuts, spices and caramelized onions. It can be cooked on the stove (and in advance) while the cauliflower is roasted in the oven. The tahini sauce, a creamy dream, can be made in a jam jar before serving. I like to add extra flair to this dish by serving the cauliflower with a knife embedded into it, like Excalibur, ready for a guest to pull out and either exclaim that they're King of the Table, or to serve the other guests with big wedges of cauliflower.

SERVES 4

cauliflower
2 tsp ground cumin
½ tsp Kashmiri chilli powder
½ tsp salt
2 tbsp canola oil
1 large cauliflower, or 2 small
   (1¾ lbs)

pilaf
1½ cups basmati rice
4 tbsp canola oil
2 large yellow onions, *halved and finely sliced*
1 tsp salt
1 tsp ground cumin
1 tsp ground coriander
¼ tsp ground black pepper
1¾ oz shelled unsalted pistachios
1¾ oz whole almonds, *roughly chopped*
¾ oz fresh cilantro, *finely chopped*
¾ oz fresh flat-leaf parsley, *finely chopped*

tahini sauce
4½ tbsp tahini
3 tbsp canola oil
2 tbsp lemon juice, *from 1 lemon*
½ small clove of garlic, *grated*
⅓ tsp salt

Preheat the oven to 400°F. In a small bowl, mix the cumin, chilli powder, ½ teaspoon of salt and 2 tablespoons of oil until you have a smooth paste.

Trim some of the leaves off the cauliflower, and cut the base so it sits flat. Rub with the spice paste and place in a high-sided baking sheet. Pour ½ cup of warm water into the bottom of the pan and roast for 1 hour, until golden and tender (check by prodding with a skewer), then remove and set aside.

While the cauliflower is roasting, wash the rice really well in a sieve, until the water runs clear, then drain, put in a bowl, pour over warm water to cover and leave to one side.

Put ¼ cup of oil into a large lidded saucepan over a medium heat and, when hot, add the onions and salt. Sauté for 12 minutes, stirring occasionally, until soft and dark. Add the spices, cook for a minute, then add the pistachios and almonds and stir to coat. Drain the rice well, then add to the onions, along with 1¾ cups of just-boiled water, and clap on the lid. Bring to a boil, then turn down the heat to the lowest setting and cook for 12 minutes. Take off the heat, keep the lid on and leave to steam.

While the rice settles, make the tahini sauce. Put everything into a jam jar or similar, add ¼ cup of water, then shake like a person possessed until you have an emulsified sauce: it should be like heavy (whipping) cream and pourable; if too thick, add more water; too thin, more tahini. Check the seasoning and adjust the salt and lemon juice if need be.

To serve, stir the herbs through the rice, then tip out onto a platter and top with the cauliflower head(s). Pour the tahini sauce into a pitcher. Stick a sharp knife in the cauliflower and encourage guests to help themselves to rice, a wedge of cauliflower and a healthy pouring of tahini sauce.

V/GF   PREP 5 mins / COOK 1 hr 15 mins

Gujarati potato and cabbage curry

This recipe is an ancient dish that my ancestors cooked over wooden fires in their village on the Kathiawar peninsula in Gujarat, western India. It's also something I ate regularly when I got home from school in Lincolnshire, while sitting in front of the telly and watching *Neighbours*, as well as something I wanted to eat almost every day when I was pregnant. It might be simple and cheap, but it's also delicious and wholesome, and deserves to continue for many more generations.

SERVES 4

1¾ lbs Yukon Gold potatoes,
   peeled and cut into 1-inch cubes
salt and ground black pepper
3 tbsp canola oil
a pinch of fenugreek seeds
½ tsp black mustard seeds
1 tsp cumin seeds
1 large yellow onion, *finely chopped*
4 cloves of garlic, *finely chopped*
½ a can (7 oz) of plum tomatoes *in their juice*
1 lb green cabbage (½ a large one), *shredded*
1 tsp ground coriander
⅓ tsp ground turmeric
1½ tsp Kashmiri chilli powder

to serve
store-bought or homemade chapattis *(p 307)*
plain Greek or dairy-free yogurt
a handful of fresh cilantro, *leaves chopped*

Put the potatoes into a pan, cover with cold water, add a teaspoon of salt and bring to a boil. Cook for 15 minutes, or until tender, then drain and leave to steam.

While the potatoes are cooking, heat the oil over a medium heat in a large frying pan for which you have a lid. Once it's very hot, add the fenugreek, mustard and cumin seeds and, when they start to crackle, stir in the onion and fry for 6 minutes, until soft. Add the garlic, cook for 2 minutes, then add the tomatoes, tipping them in with one hand and crushing them with the other before they hit the pan. Cook until the tomatoes become concentrated and paste-like and the oil floats to the top – 8 to 10 minutes.

Turn up the heat, add the cabbage and stir until well coated in the tomato mixture, then cover the pan and leave to cook for about 10 minutes, stirring infrequently, so the cabbage caramelizes a little while it softens.

When the cabbage is soft, fold in the potatoes, the ground spices and 1½ teaspoons of salt, and mix gently, so the potatoes don't break up too much. Add 1 cup of lukewarm water bit by bit, stirring after each addition, and leave to cook down, lid off, for 5 minutes, until the liquid thickens into a sauce. Check and adjust the seasoning if need be, then take off the heat.

Serve generous helpings of the curry with warmed chapattis, a large spoonful of yogurt and a handful of fresh cilantro.

Sprout and chilli peanut noodles

As a new immigrant to this country in 1972, my mother, Nita, never inherited the idea that Brussels sprouts were a mandatory, and sometimes unloved, part of Christmas dinner. She just thought of them as beautiful tiny cabbages and would squeal with delight when they came into season. We have cooked them every which way ever since.

NOTE If you have a food processor with a slicer blade, use that, but remember that shredding sprouts by hand and occasionally throwing them at people is a proven form of stress relief. I like Lee Kum Kee's fiery Chiu Chow chilli oil in this recipe, but use whatever you have.

SERVES 4

- 1–2 tbsp chilli oil and sediment, *plus extra to serve*
- 1½ tbsp white wine vinegar
- 3 tbsp toasted sesame oil
- 3 tbsp light soy sauce
- 1 tbsp toasted black sesame seeds, *plus more to decorate*
- ¼ cup salted peanuts, *finely chopped, plus more to decorate*
- 6 scallions, *whites and greens separated, finely sliced*
- 7 oz whole wheat noodles
- 3 cloves of garlic, *crushed*
- 1 lb Brussels sprouts, *finely shredded*
- salt

First, make the chilli sauce. Put ½ to 1 tablespoon of chilli sediment from the bottom of the jar into a small bowl and add ½ to 1 tablespoon of the chilli oil (depending on how hot you like it). Add the vinegar, 2 tablespoons of sesame oil, the soy sauce, sesame seeds, peanuts and a small handful of the greens from the scallions, then mix and set aside.

Cook the noodles according to the package instructions, making sure you wiggle them with a fork while they're cooking to separate them. Drain and rinse with cold water until cooled, then drain again and set aside.

To cook the sprouts, put a tablespoon of sesame oil into a large frying pan over a medium heat and, when hot, add the garlic and the scallion whites. Fry for 2 minutes, then add the sprouts and crank up the heat to high. Hard-fry the sprouts for 4 to 5 minutes, until charred and tender, then add the noodles and the sauce. Gently mix together (I find a spaghetti spoon useful for this) and taste, adding salt if need be.

To serve, heap generously onto plates and sprinkle over the reserved scallion greens, some more sesame seeds and chopped peanuts – and more chilli oil if you like.

Broccoli and other brassicas

Broccolini, tofu and kimchi stew

Homemade isn't always better. Especially when we're talking about Asian pantry ingredients like kimchi and gochujang, both used in this recipe. These ingredients take practised hands and years of knowledge to make. Plus they're fairly easy to buy now and, once bought, they obediently sit in the cupboard or fridge like sleeping giants, ready to deploy big and instant flavor. This stew is my take on the popular Korean dish *kimchi jjigae*, which is savory, tangy, warming, and greater than the sum of its parts – happily, parts mostly pre-made.

N O T E   Gochujang is a sweet and moderately hot Korean red pepper paste that can be found in most major supermarkets.

SERVES 4

3 tbsp canola oil
1 yellow onion, *finely chopped*
2 cloves of garlic, *crushed*
½ x ½ inch ginger, *finely grated*
10 oz good-quality kimchi
1 tbsp gochujang paste
1 tbsp honey or agave syrup
7 oz oyster mushrooms, *torn into strips*
4 cups vegetable stock
14 oz extra-firm tofu, *drained and cut into ¼-inch slices*
8½ oz broccolini, *halved lengthways*
salt
2 scallions, *finely shredded lengthways*
cooked jasmine rice *(p 304), to serve*

Heat the oil in a casserole dish over a medium heat and, when hot, add the onion and fry for 8 minutes, until soft. Stir in the garlic, ginger and kimchi, fry until the kimchi starts to caramelize – about 10 minutes – then stir in the gochujang and honey or agave syrup. Add the oyster mushrooms to the pot and fry for 3 minutes.

Pour in the stock, bring to a boil, then turn down the heat to a whisper and simmer for 10 minutes, until it tastes like all the flavors have come together.

Layer the tofu slices in a fan shape on one side of the pot and arrange the broccolini on the other side, then prod both to submerge them slightly in the hot liquid. Leave to cook for another 6 to 8 minutes, or until the broccolini is tender, then check the seasoning – add salt, if need be.

Either keep in the pot or transfer to a serving dish, scatter over the shredded scallions and serve with bowls of steamed jasmine rice.

Tandoori cauliflower with cilantro and cashew sauce

The secret to delicious tandoori food isn't the clay oven, it's the yogurt. It acts like a protective jacket for the spices in the marinade, allowing them to perform their magic without burning. At the same time, the yogurt caramelizes as it cooks, transforming it into something on the flavor spectrum toward heaven or cheese – perhaps the same thing.

NOTE   You'll need a blender for this recipe and some naan and some pickles alongside.

SERVES 4

pickles and sauce
½ red onion, *very finely sliced*
¼ cup lemon juice, *from 2 lemons*
salt
⅔ cup roasted unsalted cashews
3½ oz fresh cilantro, *roughly chopped*
¾ tsp superfine sugar
3 green finger (or serrano) chillies, *chopped*
2 tbsp canola oil

tandoori cauliflower
1¾ cups plain Greek yogurt
2 tbsp lemon juice, *from 1 lemon*
5 cloves of garlic, *crushed*
¾ x ¾ inch ginger, *grated*
¾ tsp ground turmeric
2 tsp Kashmiri chilli powder
2 tsp salt
1½ tsp garam masala
4 tbsp canola oil
2 tsp Colman's English mustard
2 large cauliflowers (3½ lbs), *trimmed*

store-bought or homemade hot, buttered naan *(p 306), to serve*

First, make the pickles. Place the onion in a small bowl, add 2 tablespoons of lemon juice and ½ teaspoon of salt, scrunch with your hands to wilt the onion a little and set aside.

Next, make the sauce. Place the cashews in a small heatproof bowl, cover with ½ cup of boiling water and leave to soak for 5 minutes, then put the cashews and their water into a blender. Add the cilantro, sugar, chillies, ½ teaspoon of salt, the oil and 2 tablespoons of lemon juice, blend until smooth, then taste and adjust the salt, lemon or chilli as you wish.

Line two large baking sheets with parchment paper and oil them lightly. Preheat the oven to 425°F.

To make the tandoori marinade, place all the ingredients except the cauliflowers in a large bowl and whisk to mix. Sit each cauliflower upright on your board and cut down its center, then, starting from the cut side, slice vertically into ½-inch-thick "steaks." You should get two to four intact steaks from each cauliflower and a lot of smaller pieces alongside.

Dip the larger steaks into the marinade to cover each nook and cranny, then shake off any extra and place on a baking sheet. Pop the remaining florets into the bowl and mix with your hands to coat well, then lift out, shake off, and place on the second sheet, leaving about ¾ inch between each piece. Put the baking sheets into the oven, near the top, and bake the florets for 20 minutes and the steaks for 25 minutes, rotating the trays after 10 minutes, until tender and blackening in spots.

To serve, spread a quarter of the cashew and cilantro sauce on each plate with the back of a spoon. Top with a cauliflower steak or two and several small florets, and scatter over the pickled onions. Eat with hot fresh buttered naan.

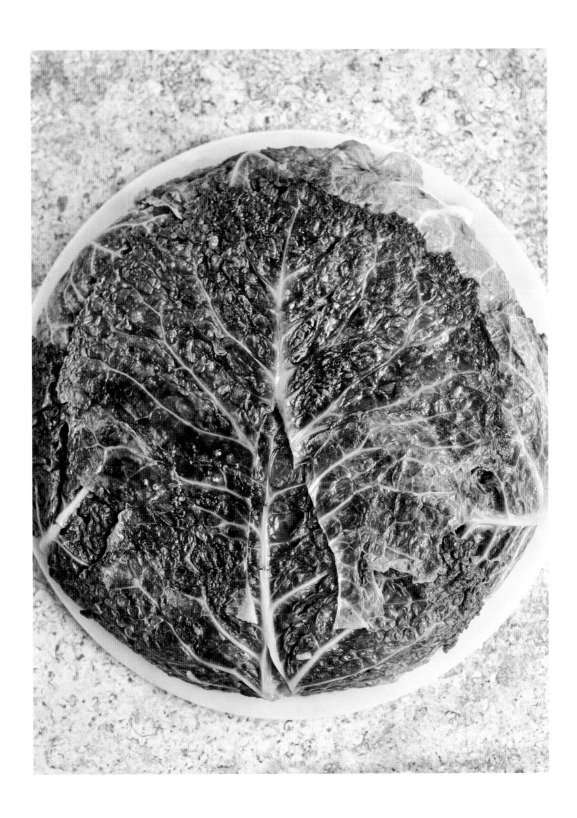

Broccoli and other brassicas

Seven treasures rice cake

This is one of those dishes that elicits an ooh from the crowd (apart from the one person who doesn't love cabbage). The treasures contained within are sticky rice, seasoned with caramelized shallots, turnips, shiitake mushrooms, ginger, garlic and spices. They're enveloped and cooked in a savoy cabbage-leaf parcel, then turned out like a jade-colored frittata. This dish can stand alone with a dipping sauce (p 233) or chilli oil alongside, but if you wanted to add to the feast, the roasted eggplant with silken tofu on p 33 works well.

NOTE Sticky rice (also known as glutinous rice) can be bought in most major supermarkets. You'll need a deep, wide nonstick lidded pan (I use my 11-inch diameter for this) and a serving board (or tray) on which to turn out the cake and serve it.

SERVES 4

2 cups Thai sticky rice

3 tbsp canola oil, *plus extra to brush*

7 large shallots (8½ oz net), *chopped*

4 cloves of garlic, *crushed*

1½ x 1½ inches ginger, *grated*

1 star anise

1 cinnamon stick

4 medium turnips (12 oz), *peeled and cut into ½-inch cubes*

6 oz fresh shiitake mushrooms, *chopped*

3 tbsp light soy sauce

1 tbsp dark soy sauce

2 tbsp Shaoxing wine

1¼ tsp salt

1 large savoy cabbage, or 2 medium (2 lbs)

Wash the rice thoroughly, cover with hand-hot water and leave to soak for 30 minutes. Meanwhile, heat the oil in the pan over a medium heat and, when hot, add the shallots, garlic, ginger, star anise and cinnamon and cook for around 12 minutes, stirring occasionally, until sticky, sweet and browning. Add the turnips, mix well and cook for 2 to 3 minutes, then add the mushrooms and cook for another 4 minutes. Stir in the soy sauces and Shaoxing wine, and cook for 10 minutes.

Scrape the mixture into a large bowl. Drain the rice, add to the bowl along with the salt, and mix. When the pan is cool enough to touch, wipe it out with paper towel, then brush a little oil on the base and sides.

Peel off the larger leaves of the cabbage and cut away the V-shaped core. Layer the leaves, curling upward, across the bottom of the pan and around the sides, overlapping them by about ¾ inch to ensure there are no gaps. Have another four large leaves ready to cover the top of the rice, like a lid.

Spoon the rice mixture into the pan and flatten it down with the back of a wooden spoon, then pour in 2 cups of cold water. Layer over more cabbage leaves until the rice is covered, and tuck them in at the sides so the parcel is as neat as possible. Put the lid on the pan, bring to a boil over a high heat and cook for 5 minutes, then turn the heat right down and simmer for 30 minutes. Turn off the heat and leave it to rest for 10 minutes.

After its resting time, remove the lid and place your board on top of the frying pan. Using a kitchen towel to protect your hands, flip the pan and board upside down to turn the cake out onto the board. Carry it triumphantly to the table, before slicing into wedges with a very sharp knife.

Drunken noodles

Imagine if there were a dish created to suit every need: a meal to celebrate anniversaries, the last day of school or to help ease a potential hangover. Well, thanks to the genius of Thai cooks, a dish for the latter does exist in the form of this recipe for *pad kee mao*, or drunken noodles. These wide, flat noodles are coated in a hot, salty and sweet basil and sour tamarind sauce, which is brought into sharp focus by some bitter radicchio and lime. They won't stop you from drinking too much, mind you. As far as I'm aware, there are still no recipes for that.

NOTE The wide, flat rice noodles or rice sticks can be found in East Asian supermarkets.

SERVES 2 generously

- **7 oz wide, flat rice noodles *or* rice sticks**
- **6 tbsp dark soy sauce**
- **2 tsp tamarind paste**
- **2 tsp palm or dark brown sugar**
- **10 oz firm tofu,** *drained*
- **¼ cup cornstarch**
- **canola oil**
- **4 cloves of garlic,** *finely sliced*
- **3 bird's-eye chillies,** *finely sliced*
- **10 oz broccolini,** *stalks cut into ½-inch-long angled pieces*
- **1 head of radicchio (12 oz),** *trimmed and cut into ¼-inch strips*
- **¾ oz fresh Thai basil,** *leaves picked*
- **1 lime,** *quartered*

Put the noodles into a large bowl and cover with cold water. Stir with tongs to separate, then set aside. Mix the soy sauce, tamarind paste and sugar in a small bowl until the sugar has dissolved, then set aside. Put a large plate lined with paper towel to one side of the stove.

Pat the tofu dry and cut into ¾-inch cubes. In a shallow bowl, coat the tofu cubes in the cornstarch. Place a large nonstick frying pan for which you have a lid on a medium heat, and add enough oil to coat the bottom of the pan. Tap off any excess cornstarch from the tofu and, once the oil is hot, fry the tofu pieces, turning them regularly with tongs or two forks, for 6 to 8 minutes, until crisp and golden all over. Using tongs, lift the tofu from the pan and transfer to the plate lined with paper towel.

Drain the noodles in a colander, and shake off any excess water. In the same pan, and using the oil left in the pan (add more, if need be), fry the garlic and chillies for a minute, then add the broccolini. Cover the pan, leave to cook for 2 minutes, add the radicchio, cover again and cook for a minute more. Remove the lid, add the tofu, noodles, sauce and basil, mix well and cook, stirring, for 3 to 4 minutes more, until the noodles are tender and cooked through.

Squeeze over the juice of half the lime. Distribute the noodles across two plates and serve with the remaining lime wedges on the side.

Knives

"Knife skills are for chefs, good knives are for cooks." – Hugh de Winton

Growing up, I was unaware of the importance of a sharp edge: the women in my family were partial to blunt paring knives. I'd watch my grandma cut onions over a bowl using her thumb in place of a chopping board. There are a few rough criss-crossed lines on her ninety-year-old thumb pads now, potentially making her a perfect criminal: unidentifiable on bio registers.

My moment of realization came one day at my parents' house when I was in my mid-twenties. Mum tuned in to QVC and I saw a man display a knife so sharp he could whip off wafer-thin slices of tomato like a Samurai, mid-air and at great speed. This was not what it looked like when I sliced tomatoes: usually the pressure of the blade forced my tomatoes to split in a place other than where I was cutting. And so began my search for a better knife.

The more serious I got about food, the more vital the knife became. Everything else you can work around, but trying to cook a decent meal without a sharp knife is near impossible – it is the one area that I would never skimp on in the kitchen. A sharp blade can make you feel like you're (literally) gliding through life's tasks with ease. It makes dicing shallots a pleasure and slicing garlic a dream. I'd be happy to put "whittling a butternut squash" down as a hobby, it releases that many endorphins.

After years of experimentation, I've come to the conclusion that there's only one knife I couldn't live without, three at a push.

My main squeeze is a sleek Japanese number called Global G-80. It doesn't have the cachet of a hand-forged saber. It was certainly sniffed at by a chef when I staged (interned) at a restaurant in Islington. The chef seemed to suggest that I was just a keen home cook and not a real chef because real chefs had badass carbon-steel knives that were always being stolen. Mine was clearly a Fisher-Price starter knife that I could leave in the kitchen overnight, because no one wanted to nick it.

Although she was right (about me being a keen home cook), a decade on and my Global knife and I are still going strong. The obvious benefit is its razor-sharp, double-bevel stainless-steel edge, which I keep samurai-sharp using a pull-through sharpener. Given that it's stainless steel, and not carbon steel, it will not rust no matter how much water or acid I throw at it, which is this low-maintenance cook's dream.

The less told but more important story is about how it just feels right in my hand, allowing it to become an extension of my arm as if the Ollivander (the wandmaker in *Harry Potter*) of the knife world had personally matched me up with this particular knife. But more likely it's because many Japanese knives are designed to be lighter than the average, which suits my delicate wrists.

The jury's out as to whether a knife is stronger in a single unit, like my Global, or semi "bolstered" with a junction that ties the blade to the handle. My knife is a bolster-less single seamless unit with a gentle slope from blade to handle, which I really like because there are no ridges on which to rub and blister a finger, even after hours of chopping.

Perhaps we're getting near the weeds now, but knives come with flat or fluted sides. I'm a huge fan of fluted because they allow air pockets to form, reducing suction when you're slicing. In practice, this means you don't have to stop every time you cut a potato, mango, avocado – anything sticky or starchy, let's say – to peel off the sticky slice before cutting again.

An excellent sidekick to the G-80 is a bright pink whippersnapper called the Victorinox Tomato Knife. Sam (he/him) of Sam and Sam at Moro introduced me to this joyful blade. It's small, nifty, and has teeth as sharp as a puppy's. It makes light work of cutting tomatoes, strawberries, shallots and, if you're my friend Meron, your interdigital folds (the bits between your fingers) too. Long live the NHS.

The third knife, in order of use, is my beloved bread knife, the Opinel curved serrated knife. The soft wooden handle makes me feel as though I am at one with the bread, and the sound and feel of the large serrated edge tearing through a crusty loaf with great friction (but few crumbs) is nearly as satisfying as the crunch of the bread in my mouth. It works like a charm on cakes and pastries too. I looked up the Amazon reviews for this knife and my favorite ones are "*****super all round jolly spot on" and "wicked sharp" – and when all is said and done, that's really all that matters.

Eat

your

greens

Miso butter greens pasta

Joshua McFadden's kale sauce has been a cult sensation, coaxing cooks around the world to eat 1 pound of Tuscan (lacinato) kale in one sitting. It's impressive on many levels: the volume of greens, the simplicity and the excellent flavor. I've made it many times, losing the Parmesan but adding some fennel seeds, chilli and miso instead. Like all the best recipes, it has taken on new life in my kitchen and, with thanks to Joshua, here's my version.

NOTE You'll need a blender and a very large pot (around 5 quarts) with a lid.

SERVES 4

¼ cup unsalted butter, *vegan or dairy*

5 cloves of garlic, *chopped*

½ tsp fennel seeds

½ tsp chilli flakes

3½ oz broccoli, *chopped*

14 oz Tuscan (lacinato) kale, *leaves stripped and sliced*

¾ tsp salt

2½ tbsp white miso paste

3 tbsp extra virgin olive oil

1 lb orecchiette

chilli oil or extra virgin olive oil, *to finish*

Melt the butter in a large pot on a medium heat. When it's bubbling, add the garlic, fennel seeds and chilli flakes, and fry, stirring, for 2 to 3 minutes, until the garlic smell changes from raw to cooked and a bit like garlic bread.

Add the broccoli, kale, salt and 1 cup of water, stir (this will be challenging, but believe in yourself), cover, turn down the heat to medium-low and cook, stirring every few minutes, for 8 to 10 minutes, until the greens have wilted and become tender.

Scrape all the contents of the kale pan into a blender or food processor, add the miso and olive oil, and blend to a smooth sauce, scraping down the sides as necessary; add a little water, if needed, to create a silky-smooth sauce (I add about ¼ cup).

Rinse out the greens pot, fill with water (do not salt it: miso is already quite salty, and you can always adjust the seasoning later) and bring to a boil. Cook the pasta according to the package instructions and, when it's got a minute to go, gently lower a large mug into the water and scoop out a mugful of the starchy cooking water.

Drain the pasta, return it to the pot, add the sauce and toss with around 6 to 8 tablespoons of the cooking water to get it to a consistency you like. Taste and add salt, if need be.

Spoon out on to a serving platter and drizzle with chilli oil or extra virgin olive oil.

Eat your greens

Tofu, coconut and green bean curry

In the tunnel between the last heat of summer and the cold air of winter (let's call it autumn?), I just want to eat curry. Not just any curry, I want something sharp and fresh that will make me feel alive – like this one, which borrows flavors from Thai cooking. It's packed with chilli, ginger, turmeric and lime, with some tofu and coconut thrown in just to round things out. I hope it will awaken your senses, clear your sinuses and put a hop in your step and skip in your hop.

SERVES 4

16 oz extra-firm tofu, *drained*
canola oil
10 oz green beans, *topped*
1 yellow onion, *finely sliced*
2 x 1½ inches ginger (1½ oz), *grated*
2 bird's-eye chillies, *finely sliced*
1½ tsp superfine sugar
½ tsp ground turmeric
1½ tsp salt
1 x 14-oz can of coconut milk
1½ tbsp lime juice, *from 1 lime*
¾ oz fresh Thai basil leaves
cooked jasmine rice *(p 304),*
  to serve

Pat the tofu dry with paper towel and cut into 1-inch cubes.

Put a large plate to one side of the stove – you'll use this later for the cooked tofu and beans. Put 3 tablespoons of oil into a large frying pan over a medium to high heat. When very hot, add the tofu and fry for 6 to 8 minutes, turning every minute or two with tongs or two forks, until golden brown all over. Keeping the pan on the heat, carefully transfer the tofu to the plate.

Add the green beans to the hot pan, shake to settle them into a single layer, and leave them to blister in the hot oil for 2 minutes. Turn over the beans, repeat on the other side and, once they're all flecked with brown, transfer to the tofu plate.

Put the pan back on the heat and add a tablespoon or so more oil. Once that's good and hot, add the onion and fry, stirring, for 6 minutes, until it's turning translucent and starting to catch at the edges. Add the ginger and chillies, stir-fry for 2 minutes, then stir in the sugar, turmeric and salt. Add the coconut milk, the cooked tofu and beans, and the lime juice, bring everything up to a simmer, then leave to cook for 5 minutes.

Stir in the Thai basil leaves, cook for a final minute, until they wilt, then stir again and taste – adjust the lime and salt if need be. Transfer the curry to a serving bowl and serve over some freshly steamed jasmine rice.

Rojak salad with avocado, tofu and tamarind

I was never fond of rojak, a Malaysian tamarind and tropical fruit salad. I found it sickly sweet, until I stumbled across the food writer Claire Thomson's version and I saw the light. Hers was more restrained, fresher and lighter. It inspired me to write my own recipe using avocado and apple. It is sour, hot and still sweet, but not too sweet.

NOTE Sambal oelek is a zingy chilli sauce used in many Indonesian and Malaysian dishes that you can buy from East Asian supermarkets and online (p 310). Once you have it, you can also make the chickpea and potato curry with quick paratha on p 190.

SERVES 2 with leftovers

2 tbsp tamarind paste
1 tbsp sambal oelek, *or to taste*
1 tbsp agave or brown rice syrup
¼ cup light soy sauce
canola oil
16 oz extra-firm tofu, *drained*
¼ green cabbage (5¼ oz), *finely shredded*
⅓ English cucumber (5¼ oz), *seeded and thinly sliced*
1¾ oz baby-leaf spinach
1 Braeburn or other crisp eating apple, *cut into ¹⁄₁₆-inch slices*
1 avocado, *pitted and cut into wedges*
a large handful of fresh mint leaves, *torn*
½ cup salted peanuts, *very finely chopped*
lime wedges, *to serve*

First, make the dressing. In a small bowl, whisk the tamarind paste, sambal oelek and syrup with 3 tablespoons of soy sauce and a tablespoon of oil. Taste the dressing, making sure you're happy with the balance of heat, sour, sweet and salt, and adjust as required.

Pat the tofu dry with paper towel and cut into 1-inch cubes. Put a tablespoon of oil into a nonstick frying pan over a medium heat and, when hot, fry the tofu cubes for 8 minutes, turning them with tongs or two forks, or until golden brown all over, then add the remaining tablespoon of soy sauce, take off the heat and tip into a serving bowl.

Add the cabbage, cucumber, spinach, apple, avocado wedges, mint leaves and half the peanuts to the bowl, then toss with clean hands. Add the dressing and mix again. Garnish with the remaining peanuts and serve with lime wedges on the side.

Sichuan green beans with tofu

When I had my first blistered and wrinkly Sichuanese dry-fried beans, I wolfed them down like McDonald's fries. They were salty, soft and crunchy, which in my book are all bywords for addictive. Traditionally, the beans would have been dry-roasted, but these days, in most restaurants at least, they're deep-fried and served with pork. In my version, I've fried them hot and hard in a little oil and served them over a soft mound of ground shiitake mushrooms and tofu.

NOTE You'll need a food processor, and a pestle and mortar (or something heavy) for bashing the peppercorns with.

SERVES 4

1 tsp Sichuan peppercorns
10 oz extra-firm tofu, *drained*
8½ oz fresh shiitake mushrooms
canola oil
14 oz green beans, *trimmed*
¾ x ¾ inch ginger, *grated*
4 cloves of garlic, *crushed*
4 scallions, *trimmed and finely chopped*
optional: 4 mild red chillies, *finely chopped*
3 tbsp Shaoxing wine
3 tbsp light soy sauce
cooked jasmine rice *(p 304), to serve*

First, bash the peppercorns to a rough powder with a pestle and mortar and put to one side. In a food processor, blitz the tofu and mushrooms until they're broken down into lentil- or chickpea-sized pieces.

Put ¼ cup of oil into a wide nonstick pan over a high heat and, once hot, carefully add the beans, keeping them in a single layer so each one is touching the base of the pan – you may find this easier to do in two batches. Leave to cook for 3 minutes, then turn using tongs or two wooden spoons. The beans and oil might spit; if they do, keep a lid cocked over them.

Cook the beans for another 6 minutes, turning them again after 3 minutes, until they look withered, blackened and blistered. Turn off the heat, then scoop the beans onto a plate, leaving the oil in the pan.

Return the pan to the heat, and add a tablespoon more oil, if need be. Add the tofu and mushroom mixture to the hot oil and cook, stirring frequently to make sure it doesn't stick to the pan, for up to 10 minutes, or until reduced and turning crisp and browned in places. Add the ginger, garlic, scallions, chillies and crushed Sichuan peppercorns, stir to mix, and cook for 3 minutes more.

Return the beans to the pan with the Shaoxing wine and soy sauce, stir for a couple of minutes, then transfer to a serving platter or plate. Serve immediately with jasmine rice.

Matar paneer

Everyone loves matar paneer, it is one of India's darlings. It's what my aunties cook when I visit. It's what is served by the truckful to guests at Gujarati weddings. And it's on every menu in every Indian restaurant (okay, most) in the UK for this reason. There are many variations of this beloved curry, but this recipe is for a North Indian–style rendition that is made extra luxurious because of the cashews blended into the sauce, bringing a velvet creaminess to which the paneer happily tips its hat.

NOTE You can replace the paneer with tofu – it works perfectly. You'll need a blender to whizz the cashews into a smooth paste.

SERVES 4

¼ cup roasted unsalted cashews
canola oil
3½ oz snow peas
5¼ oz ripe cherry tomatoes
1 large yellow onion, *finely chopped*
3 cloves of garlic, *crushed*
¾ x ¾ inch ginger, *grated*
17½ oz hard paneer, *cut into 1-inch cubes*
1 x 14-oz can of chopped tomatoes
1½ tsp salt
1 tsp ground cumin
1½ tsp ground coriander
1 tsp Kashmiri chilli powder
½ tsp ground turmeric
1 cup frozen baby peas

to serve
store-bought or homemade chapattis *(p 307)*
plain Greek or non-dairy yogurt

Place the cashews in a small heatproof bowl and pour over ½ cup of freshly boiled water. Leave for 5 minutes, then blitz the cashews and their water to a smooth paste using a blender.

Put a plate to one side of the stove (on which to put your cooked tomatoes and snow peas), and put a teaspoon of oil into a wide nonstick frying pan over a medium to high heat. When it's very hot, add the snow peas, let them crackle fiercely for a minute, then toss, leave to blister on the other side, and tip out onto the plate. Put the pan back on the heat, add another teaspoon of oil and, when hot, add the cherry tomatoes. Allow to blister for around 5 minutes, shaking the pan every now and then until blackening in spots, then tip out on top of the snow peas.

Put 2 tablespoons of oil into the same pan and turn the heat down to medium. When hot, add the onion, cook for around 8 minutes until softening, then add the garlic and ginger. Cook for a couple of minutes, stirring, then add the paneer, canned tomatoes, salt and ¾ cup (half a tomato can) of water. Mix and allow to bubble away for 10 minutes, turning the heat down a little if it starts to spit.

Add the cumin, coriander, chilli powder and turmeric, and cook, stirring, for 2 minutes. Add the cashew paste, ½ cup of water (or a quarter-canful), mix again, then return the cherry tomatoes and snow peas to the pan. Stir in the frozen baby peas and simmer for a further 5 minutes.

Serve in the pan or a large bowl with a pile of soft charred chapattis and some yogurt alongside.

Chickpea flour pancakes with coconut chutney

Food writers, like me, love to talk about the beauty of fresh ingredients all the time and advocate not fussing with them too much so they can speak for themselves. But the same could (and should) be said of excellent pantry-dwelling ingredients too. Chickpea flour (also known as gram flour) and shredded coconut might look underwhelming to start with, but with a simple bit of cooking – in this case, the addition of some fridge basics – you can create deeply savory pancakes, spiced crunchy greens and a coconut chutney that I could eat by the spoonful.

NOTE You'll need a blender and a good nonstick frying pan for the pancakes. If purple broccolini isn't in season, substitute it with green broccolini.

SERVES 4

1 cup gram (chickpea) flour
¼ tsp baking powder
¼ tsp ground turmeric
salt
1¼ cups dairy-free coconut yogurt
¾ cup unsweetened shredded
 coconut
1 green finger (or serrano) chilli,
 chopped
1 clove of garlic, *chopped*
8½ oz purple broccolini
8½ oz rainbow chard
canola oil
1 tsp black mustard seeds

First, make the chickpea pancake batter. Place the gram flour, baking powder, turmeric and ½ teaspoon of salt in a bowl and mix with a fork. Add ¼ cup of yogurt and mix and then, little by little, add 1 cup of water to the flour until you have a nice smooth batter. Leave to rest to one side.

Next, make the chutney. Blitz together the shredded coconut, the remaining 1 cup of the yogurt, the green chilli, garlic, ¾ teaspoon of salt and 4 to 5 tablespoons of water until it's lovely and smooth.

To prepare the greens, cut the florets off the broccoli and slice the stems into ¾-inch pieces, then place in a large bowl. Cut the chard stalks into ¾-inch pieces and add to the bowl, then slice the chard leaves into 1½-inch strips and leave on the chopping board.

Heat a tablespoon of oil in a large frying pan and, when hot, add the mustard seeds. Let them pop, then add the broccolini and the chard stalks. Cook for 2 minutes, then add a couple of tablespoons of water and pop a lid on. Steam for 3 minutes, add half the chutney and the chard leaves, mix, and pop the lid back on for a couple of minutes until the leaves have wilted. Taste and season if need be, then leave to rest while you cook the pancakes.

To cook the pancakes, put a drizzle of oil into a good nonstick pan over a medium heat. When hot, pour a thin layer of the batter into the pan. Leave to cook for a minute, or until golden, then flip. Cook for another minute on the other side, then slide onto a plate. Repeat with the remaining batter.

Place the pancakes on plates, spread each one with a dollop of coconut chutney, fill with greens, fold over and eat straight away.

V/GF   PREP 10 mins / COOK 35 mins

Eat your greens

Lebanese green beans and vermicelli rice

My grandma likes her green beans cooked until they're very, very soft. For years, I thought this was due to her suboptimal dental situation, but then one day I realized it was all about taste. My U-turn came on a summer's night on London's Edgware Road while inhaling a bowl of *loubieh bi zeit*: Lebanese green beans cooked slowly with onions, tomatoes and spices until they've completely surrendered. After years of cooking green beans to be crunchy and crisp, I've learned another valuable lesson: always listen to your elders.

NOTE The vermicelli here are often labeled as "vermicelli nests" in the pasta section at the supermarket.

SERVES 4

rice
1¼ cups basmati rice
2 tbsp olive oil
3½ oz vermicelli pasta nests,
    broken into roughly 2-inch pieces
2 cups vegetable stock
½ tsp salt

beans
1¾ lbs mix of runner beans and
    green beans
7 tablespoons olive oil
1 large yellow onion, or 2 small,
    diced
5 cloves of garlic, *thinly sliced*
2 lbs vine tomatoes, *chopped*
¾ tsp ground cinnamon
¾ tsp ground black pepper
¾ tsp ground cumin
1 tsp salt

plain Greek or thick dairy-free
    coconut yogurt drizzled with
    olive oil, *to serve*

Put the rice into a large bowl and cover with cold water. Mix with your hand until cloudy, drain and repeat until the water runs clear, then cover again and leave to one side to soak.

Prepare the beans: remove the strings of the runner beans if need be, using a vegetable peeler to shave off the sides, then top and tail both the green and runner beans and cut into 1½-inch pieces on an angle.

Put the 7 tablespoons of oil into a large, deep frying pan for which you have a lid and, when hot, add the onion. Cook for 10 minutes, or until soft enough to cut easily with a wooden spoon, then add the garlic. Cook for 3 minutes, then add the tomatoes and pop the lid on. Cook for around 8 to 10 minutes, until they've broken down into a tomato soup, add the spices, salt and beans, mix, then cover. Cook the beans for around 40 minutes, stirring now and then, and add a little water if they're getting dry (I added around ⅔ cup) – you want them to be a bit saucy. Take off the heat and set aside to rest.

To cook the vermicelli rice, heat the 2 tablespoons of oil over a medium heat in a saucepan for which you have a tight-fitting lid. When hot, add the broken vermicelli pieces and stir-fry for 2 minutes until a shade darker, then add the rice. Mix well to coat the grains in the oil, then add the stock and salt. Bring to a boil, put the lid on, reduce to a simmer for 12 minutes, then take off the heat and leave to rest with the lid on for another 5 minutes.

To serve, put a generous helping of vermicelli rice on each plate with some beans and a dollop of yogurt.

Persian herb, lime and kidney bean stew

I'm lucky enough to have an Armenian stepmother-in-law, Roubina, who is a passionate cook. When we meet, we talk about the joy of crispy fried onions and where to buy the best Persian walnut cookies in London (Tavazo in Finchley). During lockdown we planned a fantasy feast for when we could celebrate her birthday, and first on my list was this vegan version of *ghormeh sabzi*. With near a half-kilo of herbs, you might think it'll taste wild, but when cooked, the wildest thing about it is how deliciously tame they become.

NOTE You'll need dried limes – ideally black, but white are fine – and kasoori methi (dried fenugreek leaves). They're both available in Middle Eastern shops and online (p 310). You'll also need a food processor.

SERVES 4

1½ cups basmati rice
7 oz fresh flat-leaf parsley
7 oz fresh cilantro
7 oz baby-leaf spinach
6 tbsp olive oil
2 yellow onions, *finely chopped*
3 small leeks (10 oz), *trimmed and finely chopped*
1 tbsp kasoori methi
2 tsp salt, *plus extra for the rice*
¼ tsp ground black pepper
½ tsp ground cinnamon
½ tsp ground turmeric, *plus extra for the rice*
4 dried Iranian limes, *pricked with a fork*
2 x 15-oz cans of kidney beans in water, *drained*
2 tbsp lime juice, *from 1–2 limes*

First, wash the rice really well under cold water until it runs clear, then set aside in a bowl covered with water.

Remove and discard any thick or woody stems from the herbs, then roughly chop the herbs and the spinach, put into a food processor and whizz until super fine – you might need to do this in batches. Transfer to a bowl and set aside.

Put the oil into a big pot over a medium heat and, once hot, add the onions and leeks, and cook, stirring often, for 12 minutes, until soft and pearlescent. Add the blitzed herb and spinach mix and crumble in the kasoori methi, then cook for about 20 minutes, regularly swooshing it around the pan with a spoon, until the mix comes together in soft clumps and emits a deep, forest-like smell. Stir in the salt and spices, then add the dried limes and kidney beans, and stir to combine. Pour over 3 cups of water and the lime juice, mix again, then bring to a boil. Turn down the heat to a simmer and leave to cook gently, stirring occasionally, for about 15 minutes, until thick and stew-like.

Meanwhile, make the rice. Drain the rice well and put into a medium-sized saucepan with 2⅔ cups of fresh cold water and ¼ teaspoon each of salt and turmeric. Stir, then bring to a boil, cover, turn down the heat to a whisper and leave to cook for 12 minutes.

Take off the heat and leave to rest, still covered, for another 10 minutes. To serve, spoon the rice into shallow bowls and top with the stew— making sure you leave the limes behind in the pot so that people don't get a nasty surprise.

V/GF   PREP 10 mins / COOK 1 hr

Green tea rice with sake vegetables

During lockdown, the only way I could travel was by remembering the places I'd been to and the people I'd met there. One person who came to mind was Sanjay, who managed the Glenburn Tea Estate in Darjeeling. At dinner, he cut open a bottle of champagne using a sword, while telling a story about a battle he once had with a king cobra. But the thing that I took away from Sanjay was his love of using green tea in cooking. He smoked ingredients with it, and he used it in salads and cakes. Here, I've used it as a stock in which to cook rice, which yields results much gentler and less dramatic than Sanjay's stories.

NOTE I used matcha green tea bags but any good green tea bag will work.

SERVES 4

1¾ cups jasmine rice
2 matcha or green tea bags
1¼ tsp salt
3 tbsp canola oil
3 cloves of garlic, *cut wafer-thin*
10 scallions, *finely sliced*
8½ oz baby bok choy, *quartered*
8½ oz frozen baby peas
7 oz snow peas
¼ cup light soy sauce
¼ cup cooking sake
optional: toasted black sesame
   seeds, *to serve*

Wash the rice several times in cold water until it runs clear, then drain.

Put the tea bags and 2¼ cups of water into a medium-sized saucepan (for which you have a tight-fitting lid), bring to a boil, leave to boil for a minute, then take off the heat. Squeeze the tea bags against the side of the pan using the back of a spoon, then discard them. Add the drained rice and salt to the pan, bring back to a boil over a medium heat, then cover, turn down the heat to a whisper and leave to cook for 12 minutes. Take off the heat and, with the lid still on, set aside to rest for 10 minutes.

Meanwhile, cook the vegetables. Put the oil into a wide frying pan for which you have a lid and set over a medium to low heat. Once the oil is hot, add the garlic and scallions, and cook for 8 minutes, stirring occasionally. Add the baby bok choy, frozen baby peas, snow peas, soy sauce and sake, cover and leave to steam for 5 to 7 minutes, until tender but still vibrant green. To serve, spoon the green tea rice onto plates and follow with the vegetables. Scatter each plate with black sesame seeds if you wish.

Eat your greens

Eat your greens

Xi'an-style pappardelle with baby bok choy

"Out of adversity comes opportunity," said Benjamin Franklin, and out of one woman's failed attempt to make biang biang pulled noodles comes the decision to replace them with dried pappardelle. This recipe was inspired by the mighty hand-pulled noodles with "special sauce" served at Xi'an Impression in Highbury, London. They're so perfect, so unbeatable, and are made by experts to order, so they're never going to be the same at home. This isn't quite them, but thanks to Italy and its love for pappardelle, you can get a lot of the way there.

N O T E My go-to brand for chilli crisp is Lao Gan Ma, which along with Chinkiang vinegar, a sharp black vinegar made from fermented sticky rice, is available in East Asian shops and online (p 310). At a push, the vinegar could be substituted with a light balsamic.

SERVES 4

6½ tbsp light soy sauce

3 tbsp oil from chilli crisp, plus
   1 tbsp sediment

1½ tbsp Chinkiang vinegar

12 scallions, *greens and whites
   separated, finely sliced*

5 tbsp canola oil

6 cloves of garlic, *crushed*

14 oz dried pappardelle

3 heads of baby bok choy (13 oz),
   petals separated and cores halved

¼ tsp salt

Put the soy sauce, chilli oil, chilli crisp sediment, vinegar and scallion greens into a large bowl, mix together and set aside.

Put the canola oil into a wide frying pan, for which you have a lid, over a low to medium heat, then add the scallion whites and the garlic. Cook gently for 3 to 4 minutes, stirring often, until the garlic is pale gold. Put half the mixture into the soy sauce bowl and leave the remaining half in the pan.

Bring a large saucepan of unsalted water to a rolling boil, add the pappardelle and cook according to the package instructions, then drain. Add the pasta to the bowl containing the sauce and mix until well combined.

Put the pan with the scallion mixture back over a high heat. When hot, add the baby bok choy, salt and ¼ cup of water, and stir to mix. Place the lid on the pan and cook for 2 minutes, until tender. Turn off the heat and remove the lid.

Divide the pasta between four plates and place a quarter of the baby bok choy alongside, on each.

Coconut-braised winter greens

There's something about Mary. Chef Mary San Pablo, that is, and that something is that she cooks some exceptionally fine food of Filipino origin, with an English lilt. She runs pop-ups in London under the name of Luto, and it was at one that I first ate *laing*, a dish of coconut-milk-braised greens traditionally made with taro leaves. Mary used kale, which she cooked to silky, flavorful submission (not words I usually reserve for kale) and served over rice. I liked it so much, I wanted to eat it again, which is how this recipe came to be.

SERVES 4

3 tbsp canola oil

1 large yellow onion, *finely sliced*

4 cloves of garlic, *crushed*

1½ x 1½ inches ginger, *grated*

4 bird's-eye chillies, *finely chopped*

2 leeks (8½ oz), *trimmed and finely sliced*

14 oz Tuscan (lacinato) kale, *ribs removed and discarded, leaves shredded*

½ medium savoy cabbage (14 oz), *cored and finely shredded*

2½ tbsp brown rice miso

2 tbsp white wine vinegar

¾ tsp salt

1 tbsp light soy sauce

1 x 14-oz can of coconut milk

1¾ cups frozen peas, *thawed*

cooked jasmine rice *(p 304), to serve*

Put a large deep-sided pot on the stove over a medium heat and add the oil. When hot, add the onion and cook for 10 minutes, stirring regularly, until soft and browning. Add the garlic, ginger and chillies and cook for 3 minutes, stirring often, then add the leeks and cook for a further 5 minutes.

Stir in the chopped kale – you may need to do this in batches, to allow the leaves to wilt a little – then cook, stirring occasionally, for 5 minutes. Add the savoy cabbage and cook for 5 minutes, until the cabbage leaves are soft and bright green.

Add the miso, vinegar, salt and soy sauce, stir to mix in, then pour in the coconut milk. Fill the empty can with water, add this to the pot too, and bring everything to a boil. Pop the peas in for a final 3 to 4 minutes, just to heat through, then take off the heat and serve hot over freshly boiled rice.

Eggs

and

cheese

Eggs and cheese

Baked butter paneer

I used to eat paneer butter masala regularly with an Indian friend, Aditya, at a little place near Russell Square in London until one day something awkward happened that meant we never went back. That day, he made the error of wearing a black shirt and black trousers to dinner and, like a rugby player with the ball, was tackled a couple of times on his way to the bathroom as he was mistaken for a waiter. Aditya, this one's for you.

NOTE I should address the awkward truth that I don't use butter here but cream instead. You could, if you're a stickler for tradition (and not a heretic like me), add a big slab of butter to the finished curry. Kasoori methi are dried fenugreek leaves, which you can find in South Asian supermarkets or online (p 310). This recipe goes really well with the asparagus and cashew thoran on p 268.

SERVES 4

paneer
canola oil
17½ oz hard paneer, *cut into 1-inch cubes*
6 cloves of garlic, *crushed*
¾ x ¾ inch ginger, *finely grated*
1 tsp Kashmiri chilli powder
½ tbsp lemon juice, *from ½ lemon*
¾ tsp salt
½ tsp ground turmeric
5 tbsp plain Greek yogurt

butter sauce
1 tsp Kashmiri chilli powder
1 tsp garam masala
1 tsp ground cumin
½ tsp ground cardamom
¾ tsp salt
2 tbsp liquid honey
2 x 14-oz cans of chopped tomatoes
⅔ cup heavy (whipping) cream
1½ tbsp kasoori methi

to serve
naan *(p 306)*
optional: a slab of butter

Preheat the oven to 425°F and line a deep baking sheet or baking dish (roughly 12 x 8 inches) with nonstick parchment paper. Brush the paper with a little oil.

Put the paneer cubes into a mixing bowl and add half the garlic, half the ginger and then the chilli powder, lemon juice, salt, turmeric and yogurt. Mix well, tip onto the baking sheet and bake for 25 minutes, or until the paneer is crisp and starting to blacken ever so slightly at the edges.

Take the baking sheet out of the oven and very carefully remove the parchment paper, leaving the paneer on the baking sheet. Add 3 tablespoons of oil and the remaining ginger and garlic, stir to coat the paneer in the garlicky oil, then add the spices for the butter sauce, the salt and the honey. Stir to mix, then tip in the tomatoes, making sure the paneer is completely covered, and pop back in the oven for 30 minutes.

Remove the baking sheet, stir through the cream, crumble over the kasoori methi, then stir again and pop back in the oven for 10 minutes. Remove the baking sheet once more, stir in the butter now if you'd like, then serve straight from the pan with hot naan.

Sticky mango and lime paneer naans

Good things come in threes: buses, the little pigs and Destiny's Child. I'm adding paneer, naan and mango chutney to that list.

NOTE Don't be put off by the list of ingredients: there's very little cooking to be done here.

SERVES 4

5 tbsp plain Greek yogurt

5 tbsp mayonnaise

½ tbsp mild curry powder

3½ tbsp mango chutney (I like Geeta's)

½ red cabbage (8½ oz), core removed, the rest very finely shredded

salt

2 limes: 1 juiced to get 2 tbsp, the other quartered

2 cloves of garlic, crushed

1 tbsp gram (chickpea) flour

1 tbsp canola oil

17½ oz hard paneer, cut into 1-inch cubes

4 store-bought naan or flatbreads

1 oz fresh mint, leaves picked

First, make the curried mayo. Put the yogurt, mayonnaise, curry powder and a tablespoon of mango chutney into a bowl, mix well and leave to one side.

Next, place the shredded cabbage in a bowl with ½ teaspoon of salt, then scrunch with clean hands until wilted. (If you get red hands, scrub them with the inside of the juiced lime to remove the color.)

For the sticky mango and lime glaze, put the lime juice, 2½ tablespoons of mango chutney, the garlic, gram flour, a teaspoon of salt and 3 tablespoons of water into a bowl and stir well.

Put the oil into a frying pan over a medium to high heat. When hot, fry the paneer, turning every minute or so to brown each side, for around 5 minutes. Turn the heat down, add the mango and lime glaze and cook for 3 to 4 minutes, stirring, until the glaze goes sticky and coats the paneer cubes.

Heat the naan or flatbreads (I zap them in the microwave), then slather over the curry mayonnaise, scatter over the cabbage, cover with the paneer and sprinkle with some mint leaves. Squeeze over some more lime, then roll up and eat.

Soy butter eggs with nori

Eggs over rice, for me, are a panacea for all woes. Bad traffic, bad weather, the printer not working, rising sea levels or accidentally stepping on tiny Lego pieces with bare feet – anything that life throws at me on the regular. While these eggs don't make my problems disappear, they do give me comfort, pleasure and more strength to fight a little harder.

This is tangentially based on the Korean home cook's favorite, gyeran bap. In my version I've flavored the rice with sesame oil, fried the eggs, and topped them with buttery soy and mirin-soaked nori.

NOTE Nori, a dried edible seaweed, is often used to wrap sushi and can be called "sushi nori" – you can find it in larger supermarkets.

SERVES 2

1 cup short-grain or sushi rice
2½ tbsp light soy sauce
2 tbsp mirin
2 tbsp toasted sesame oil
1 sheet of nori, *ripped into irregular pieces*
3 tbsp unsalted butter, *cubed*
1 tbsp canola oil
2–4 eggs *(depending on appetite)*

Place the rice in a medium-sized saucepan for which you have a tight-fitting lid and cover with lukewarm water. Agitate the rice with your hand until the water becomes cloudy, then drain and repeat, until the water runs clear. Cover with warm water and leave to soak for 5 minutes, then drain again and put the rice back into the saucepan with 1¼ cups of water over a medium heat. Put the lid on and bring the rice to a boil, then immediately turn the heat down and simmer for 10 minutes. After this time, turn off the heat, keep the lid on and leave to rest for 10 minutes, while you prepare the eggs.

For the eggs, whip out your fish spatula or slotted spoon and place a plate by the side of the stove. Pour the soy sauce, mirin and sesame oil into a small bowl and put the nori pieces on top of the liquid.

Put the butter and canola oil into a wide nonstick frying pan over a medium heat. When it starts to foam, crack in the eggs. I like to tip the pan gently from side to side to get the butter over the tops of the eggs, or baste them using a spoon. Cook for 3 to 3½ minutes if you like a runny yolk, or until they're as you like them, then take off the heat and transfer to the plate using the slotted spoon. Pour the soy sauce mixture and nori into the hot pan and mix.

To serve, distribute the rice between two bowls, add one or two eggs to each bowl and pour the buttery soy juices and nori over the top. Eat immediately.

PREP 5 mins / COOK 25 mins

Marbled egg omelet with nam pla

Minutes after landing in Bangkok, I took a tuk-tuk forty minutes out of the city to a neighborhood restaurant called Baan Pee Lek, where I instantly fell in love, not with a man, but with an omelet. It was what most other eggs could only dream of becoming: ribboned white and gold, wrinkled, and wobbly in the center. As simple as it is, for me it is the beating heart of this book. It's easy, beautiful and really, truly delicious. The nam pla sauce adds another string to this omelet's bow, allowing it to mix more easily with rice and become a complete meal.

NOTE Make the rice first if you're eating it alongside. You'll need a good nonstick pan for which you have a lid. You'll also need a quality vegan fish sauce such as Tofuna Fysh Sauce.

SERVES 2

1 bird's-eye chilli, *finely sliced*
2½ tbsp vegan fish sauce
1 tbsp lime juice, *from 1 lime*
8 large eggs
¼ cup canola oil
¼ tsp salt

to serve

cooked jasmine rice *(p 304)*
vegan fish sauce
mayonnaise, *ideally Kewpie*

First, make the nam pla: put the chilli, 2 tablespoons of vegan fish sauce and the lime juice into a little bowl and stir, then set aside.

To make the omelet, crack the eggs into a bowl and add ½ tablespoon of vegan fish sauce and the salt. Pierce the yolks with a fork, then gently mix so that the yolks and whites are ribboned or marbled together.

Put the oil into a wide nonstick pan, for which you have a lid, over a medium heat and have a wooden spoon on standby. Check the temperature of the oil by dipping the wooden spoon into the pan: when bubbles form around the tip of the spoon, the oil is hot enough.

Pour the eggs into the pan and, with a wooden spoon, and treating the pan as if it were a clockface, push the wet egg mixture into the center of the pan at the 1, 2, 3 (and so on) hour marks, continuing in a clockwise direction until you're back to where you started. Do this twice in fairly quick succession (it should take around 2 minutes), then pop the lid on for the final 30 seconds to just cook the egg on top.

Cut into quarters and serve over freshly cooked rice with the nam pla, extra vegan fish sauce and Kewpie mayonnaise on the side.

Eggs and cheese

Cheddar and gochujang cornbread

In 2004, after finishing uni, I moved into a tiny flat in Islington with a friend, Julie. We were both working long hours in poorly paid jobs and to make things worse, I was fired. To cheer me up Julie treated me to dinner at a new place we'd seen called Ottolenghi. I ordered a jalapeño and cheese cornbread and it blew my mind. I was so rapturous about it, the waitress gave me some to take home and Yotam's email address to ask for the recipe. I never emailed him, but it turned my bad day around and now I'm thankful for the twists in life that have led to me writing my own cornbread recipe here, in homage to the original gangster.

NOTE This works as a light summer meal, but fried eggs, sour cream and avocado would pad it out nicely. You'll need an 11-inch ovenproof sauté or frying pan for this recipe.

SERVES 4–6

cornbread
1 cup all-purpose flour
1¼ cups fine cornmeal
2 tsp baking powder
½ tsp baking soda
2 tbsp superfine sugar
1½ tsp salt
1½ cups plain Greek yogurt
3 cloves of garlic, *crushed*
4 large eggs
3 tbsp gochujang paste
9 tbsp unsalted butter, *melted, plus extra to grease*
7 oz sharp Cheddar, *grated*

pickled corn
canola oil
1 red onion, *finely sliced*
2 green finger (or serrano) chillies, *finely chopped*
2 tbsp white wine vinegar
¾ tsp salt
1⅓ cups frozen corn, *thawed*
1 tbsp raw black sesame seeds
½ oz fresh cilantro, *chopped*

optional: sour cream, fried eggs and avocado, *to serve*

Preheat the oven to 400°F and generously grease your pan with butter.

Put the flour, cornmeal, baking powder, baking soda, sugar and salt into a large bowl and whisk well. Next, put the Greek yogurt, garlic, eggs, gochujang, melted butter and half the grated Cheddar into a large pitcher or bowl and mix. Tip the wet ingredients into the dry, stir well, then pour into the greased pan and sprinkle over the remaining grated Cheddar. Bake in the oven for 30 minutes, or until the cheese is golden and a skewer inserted into the center of the bread comes out clean.

Meanwhile, make the pickled corn. Put a tablespoon of oil into a large frying pan over a medium to high heat and, when hot, add the onion and chillies and fry for 4 to 5 minutes. Stir in a tablespoon of vinegar and ½ teaspoon of salt, then transfer to a bowl. Put another tablespoon of oil into the pan, add the corn and cook for 6 to 8 minutes, stirring only once or twice to allow the kernels to catch and blacken a bit. Return the onion to the pan and stir in another tablespoon of vinegar, the sesame seeds and ¼ teaspoon of salt. Take off the heat and stir through the cilantro.

When the cornbread is ready, remove from the oven and let it cool for a few minutes. Either serve it straight from the pan or turn it out by placing a chopping board or large flat plate over the top of the pan and, using oven gloves, flipping the cornbread over (it will now be upside down). You can then flip the cornbread over onto your serving plate. Spoon the pickled corn salad into the middle of the cornbread, slice and serve warm with avocado, fried eggs and a dollop of sour cream if you wish.

Fried egg salad

This is one of the fastest ways to cook an egg in the East: the tops of the eggs are basted using the hot oil from the bottom of the pan, meaning there's no waiting for the runny bit around the yolks to cook. As a bonus, you create fantastic texture: crisp, golden, lacy and bubbled whites, and barely cooked yolks. But the best bit about this recipe isn't even the speed, or the texture, it's the joy of the hot and sour Thai dressing, which mixes with the yolks and rice in the most excellent way.

NOTE   I'd recommend cooking the jasmine rice first to eat alongside; it will stay warm for up to an hour before eating. Not all vegan fish sauces are equal (Tofuna makes a good one); use the best-quality one you can find.

SERVES 2

2½ tbsp lime juice, *from 2–3 limes*

2½ tbsp vegan fish sauce

2½ tsp soft light brown or palm sugar

1 clove of garlic, *crushed*

1 bird's-eye chilli, *finely sliced*

1 scallion, *finely sliced*

2 large shallots (2½ oz net), *halved lengthways, sliced into long thin strips*

canola or sunflower oil

4 eggs

a handful of fresh cilantro, *leaves picked*

cooked jasmine rice *(p 304),* *to serve*

First, make the dressing. Put the lime juice, vegan fish sauce and sugar into a small bowl and mix together until the sugar dissolves. Add the garlic, chilli, scallion, shallots and 1½ tablespoons of water, mix again and set aside.

Next, line a plate with paper towel, and get a fish spatula or slotted spoon ready.

To fry your eggs, pour ¼ inch of oil into a medium nonstick frying pan and set it over a medium heat. When the oil is too hot to hold a hand over at 4 inches away, gently break in 2 eggs. They might spit: beware! Feel free to turn the heat down a little if it's too intense. The eggs should bubble up. Cook for 1 to 1½ minutes, basting the yolks carefully with the hot oil so that the translucent egg turns white and the edges are lacy, golden and crisp. (This timing will give you a very runny yolk, but for a firmer yolk, cook for 2 minutes.) Transfer the eggs to your lined plate using the slotted spoon, then repeat with the remaining eggs.

When you've cooked all the eggs, transfer them to a lipped serving plate using the slotted spoon and pour over the dressing. Scatter over the cilantro and serve immediately with freshly steamed jasmine rice.

DF/GF   PREP 8 mins / COOK 10 mins

Malabar Hill eggs with tomato chutney

Some of my best friends in Mumbai are Parsis, descendants of Persian Zoroastrians who immigrated to India thousands of years ago. Parsis are famously eccentric and famously egg-obsessed. Their obsession extends beyond the kitchen: *achoo-meechoo*, for example, is a custom where the egg is waved around the person's head (six times clockwise, once anti-clockwise), then broken to ward away evil. When it comes to cooking eggs, a Parsi favorite is *kanda papeta par eeda*, or eggs on potatoes, something I ate when staying with friends in Malabar Hill and that inspired this recipe.

NOTE A food processor with a large grater attachment will make light work of grating the potatoes, although you could use a box grater if you have the stamina. You'll need a 16- x 12-inch baking sheet.

SERVES 2–4

tomato chutney
12 oz ripe tomatoes, *finely chopped*
1 tbsp lime juice, *from 1 lime*
1 tsp chipotle chilli flakes, *ground with a pestle and mortar*
3 cloves of garlic, *crushed*
¾ tsp salt

potatoes and eggs
canola oil
2 lbs Yukon Gold potatoes, *washed*
1½ tsp salt
1 yellow onion, *finely sliced*
1 tsp ground cumin
½ tsp ground turmeric
4 large eggs

to serve
optional: fresh cilantro, *leaves picked*
flaky sea salt

Preheat the oven to 400°F, then line a baking sheet with parchment paper and grease with a little canola oil.

Make the tomato chutney first. Put all the ingredients for it into a serving bowl, mix really well and leave to one side.

Next, grate the potatoes in the food processor, then add to a large bowl along with a teaspoon of salt, mix with your hands and leave for 5 minutes.

Place the potatoes on a clean, thin kitchen towel and scoop up the edges together, then wring the towel until you can't squeeze out any more water. Pop the potatoes back into the bowl and add the onion, cumin, turmeric, ¼ cup of oil and ½ teaspoon of salt. Mix really well with a spoon and tip out onto the baking sheet, spreading the mixture out to the edges. Put into the oven and cook for 40 minutes.

Remove the baking sheet from the oven and, using the back of a large spoon, make four shallow indents in the potato mixture. Gently and carefully crack an egg into each indent, then put back into the oven for 8 to 10 minutes, or until the whites are just set, the yolks are still runny (if that is how you like your eggs) and the potatoes are golden and crispy.

While still on the baking sheet, scatter over the cilantro leaves if using and crumble a little sea salt over the eggs. Slice up, divide between your plates and eat straight away with the chutney alongside.

GF/DF   PREP 5 mins / COOK 1 hr 15 mins

Taipei crispy pancakes with Gruyère and kimchi

One of Taipei's most popular breakfast eats – which I prefer to eat for dinner – is *dan bing*, meaning "egg pancake": a part-crispy, part-chewy pancake containing a thin layer of egg and anything else you could wish for: corn, cheese, scallions – the sky's the limit.

NOTE This recipe makes 4 to 5 pancakes. Divide the egg mixture by the amount of pancakes you end up making. Usually, dan bing is served with a sweet soy sauce. If you can't find it, mix 2 tablespoons of dark soy sauce with 2 tablespoons of light agave or brown rice syrup.

SERVES 2

pancakes
⅔ cup all-purpose flour
3 tbsp cornstarch
¼ tsp salt
1 large egg
canola oil

filling
3½ oz kimchi, *drained and chopped*
3½ oz Gruyère, *grated*
4 large eggs
½ tsp white pepper
½ tsp salt
5 scallions, *finely chopped*

sweet soy sauce, *to serve*

First, make the pancake batter. Put the flour, cornstarch and salt into a mixing bowl and whisk to mix. Add the egg and, little by little, pour in ¾ cup + 3 tablespoons of warm water, whisking until smooth.

Next, make the filling. Put the kimchi and grated Gruyère into a separate bowl and mix. Crack the eggs into a pitcher, and add the pepper, salt and almost all of the scallions, reserving a tablespoonful to decorate the pancakes with later. Mix well.

Heat a teaspoon of oil in a nonstick frying or pancake pan over a medium to high heat and, when hot, add a ladleful or so of batter and rotate the pan, so that the batter coats the bottom. Cook for around a minute, until the pancake no longer looks translucent, then flip and cook for 30 seconds. Pop on a plate and repeat with the remaining batter, topping up the oil when you can no longer see a trace of it on the pan.

To cook the dan bing, heat a teaspoon of oil in the same pan over a medium heat until hot. Depending on whether you have four or five pancakes, pour in a quarter or a fifth of the egg mixture and let it bubble. When it's cooked at the edges but still raw in the middle, lay one pancake on top of it. Let it cook for around 30 seconds, until the egg has cooked and you can turn it over with a spatula, then sprinkle a quarter, or a fifth, of the kimchi-Gruyère mixture in a line down the middle.

Roll up the pancake. I like to use two spatulas to do this: I start at one side and keep folding the pancake over. Cook the rolled pancake in the pan for a couple of minutes, or until the outside is blistering and you suspect the cheese is oozy in the middle. Slide onto a plate and repeat. To serve, cut the dan bing into 1 to 1½-inch slices, scatter over the remaining scallions and drizzle over the sweet soy.

Eggs and cheese

Chilli paneer, Korean style

From India you have one of the world's best fryable cheeses in the form of paneer, and from Korea, one of the best chilli pastes. It was just a matter of time before these two had a kitchen liaison.

NOTE Paneer and gochujang, the sweet, hot and funky Korean red pepper paste, are available in most major supermarkets. Make the rice first if you're eating it alongside.

SERVES 4

2 tbsp gochujang paste
1½ tbsp brown rice syrup or honey
2 tbsp light soy sauce
2 tbsp toasted sesame oil
1½ tsp white wine vinegar
canola oil
1 lb hard paneer, *cut into 1-inch cubes*
4 cloves of garlic, *crushed*
4 scallions, *finely sliced*
¾ x ¾ inch ginger, *thinly matchsticked*
10 oz baby-leaf or regular greens, *cut into ½-inch ribbons*
cooked short-grain rice *(p 305), to serve*

First, make the sauce. Put the gochujang and brown rice syrup or honey into a medium-sized bowl, mix, then add the soy sauce, sesame oil, vinegar and 3 tablespoons of water and mix again. Leave to one side.

Put 2 tablespoons of canola oil into a large nonstick frying pan over a medium heat and, when hot, add the paneer and have a spatula on hand. Turn the paneer every minute or so for around 6 minutes, until the color of the cubes ranges from pale to burnished gold. Scoop out into a bowl, leaving the oil in the pan if you can.

Return the pan to the heat and add a tablespoon of canola oil if need be. When hot, add the garlic, scallions and ginger, stir-fry for a minute, then add the paneer and the gochujang sauce. Let it bubble away for 2 minutes, then add the greens, a handful at a time if they're threatening to spill out of the pan. Fry, mixing every now and then, for 6 to 8 minutes, until the greens are dark, rich and oily and there's a glaze-like sauce over both the greens and the paneer.

Spoon the paneer and rice into two separate serving bowls, furnish both with spoons and encourage people to help themselves.

Maharani salad

Maharani means "Queen" in Hindi. Go ahead and treat yourself, Your Highness.

NOTE This salad is best served fresh out of the oven when the paneer is soft and hot.

SERVES 2 for dinner, with leftovers

1½ tsp hot smoked paprika

1 tsp ground coriander

1 tsp ground cumin

½ tsp ground turmeric

canola oil

salt

2 lbs cauliflower, *leaves and stem removed*

1 large red onion, *cut into ¾-inch wedges*

10 oz broccolini, *woody ends removed*

8½ oz hard paneer, *cut into ½-inch-thick slices, widthways*

½ cup blanched almonds, *roughly chopped*

1½ tbsp lemon juice, *from 1 lemon*

3 to 3½ oz pea sprouts or salad leaves

Preheat the oven to 425°F.

Put the paprika, coriander, cumin and turmeric into a small bowl and mix together.

Pour 3 tablespoons of oil into a large mixing bowl, add 2 teaspoons of the spice mix and ½ teaspoon of salt and stir to mix.

Break the cauliflower into florets no larger than 1½ inches and add them to the mixing bowl, then add the red onion and toss to coat in the spice oil. Tip these out onto a large roasting pan in a single layer (keeping the bowl to one side) and roast in the hot oven for 30 minutes, or until slightly tender and beginning to char.

Meanwhile, put the broccolini, paneer and almonds into the same mixing bowl, add 2 tablespoons of oil, the remaining spices and ½ teaspoon of salt and mix really well. Tip these out onto a second pan and roast for the last 10 minutes of the cauliflower cooking time.

When the vegetables are tender and burnished, leave to cool for 5 minutes, then tip the vegetables and paneer onto one pan. Drizzle with oil, add the lemon juice and a final ¼ teaspoon of salt, then mix in the pea sprouts or salad leaves. Divide the salad between two plates and eat straight away.

GF   PREP 5 mins / COOK 45 mins

Eggs and cheese

Golden mile pizza

Would you like Indian tonight? Or pizza? With this pizza, you can have both. This is written in memory of the beloved pizza of my youth, a vegetarian number that I ate at one of the many Indian restaurants on Leicester's Golden Mile, Belgrave Road, circa 1990 with my cousins, before drinking lots of Rubicon mango juice and doing handbrake turns in a nearby car park.

NOTE For ease, the dough comes together in 5 minutes in a food processor and proofs overnight in the fridge. You'll need to start the day before, but it can be kept in the fridge for up to five days. You'll need two large containers or bowls to proof the dough, a 16- x 12-inch baking sheet and chaat masala, which you can buy in any Indian supermarket or online (p 310).

MAKES 2 large pizzas, to feed 4

pizza dough
5 cups bread flour, *plus extra to dust*
1 tbsp superfine sugar
2 tsp salt
¼ oz or 2 tsp instant dry yeast
3 tbsp canola oil, *plus extra for greasing*

tomato sauce
1 tbsp canola oil
2 cloves of garlic, *crushed*
1 x 14-oz can of chopped tomatoes
½ tsp Kashmiri chilli powder
2 tbsp tomato ketchup
½ tsp salt

toppings
¼ cup canola oil
1 tbsp chaat masala
2 green finger (or serrano) chillies, *finely chopped*
7 oz pre-grated (i.e., low moisture) mozzarella
10 oz cherry tomatoes, *halved*
¾ cup corn niblets, *frozen and thawed or canned and drained*
1 green bell pepper, *cut into ½-inch slices*
½ red onion, *cut into ¼-inch slices*
2 x 4½-oz balls of mozzarella, *drained and torn*

Grease the two tubs or bowls for storing your dough.

To make the dough, put the flour, sugar, salt and yeast into a food processor and pulse a few times until well mixed. Add the canola oil and 2 cups of lukewarm water, pulse until the dough forms a ball and continue to mix for another 20 seconds. Tip the dough out onto a lightly floured surface and knead for 5 minutes, until you have a smooth ball. Divide the dough into two equal balls and pop into the containers. Cover with a lid or plastic wrap and place in the fridge for at least a day and up to five.

To make the tomato sauce, put the oil into a saucepan over a medium heat. When hot, add the garlic and cook for a minute, then add the chopped tomatoes and chilli powder. Cook for 10 minutes, then add the ketchup and salt, take off the heat, leave to cool and refrigerate until ready to use.

On the day you want to make your pizza, remove the dough from the fridge at least an hour before baking. Fifteen minutes before baking your pizza, preheat the oven to its hottest setting and put an oven rack in the center. Lay your toppings out in front of you. To make the chilli oil, put the oil, chaat masala and chillies into a small bowl and stir to mix.

Grease a baking sheet well. Gently push and stretch one ball of dough into the baking sheet evenly until it reaches the corners, being careful not to push out all the air bubbles, especially at the edges. Spread half the tomato sauce evenly over the base, then scatter over half of the toppings in this order: the grated mozzarella, the cherry tomatoes, corn, green pepper, onion and finally the fresh mozzarella. Bake for 12 to 15 minutes, until the cheese is bubbling, then remove. Drizzle over the chilli oil, slice the pizza into eight pieces and tuck in. Repeat with the remaining dough and toppings.

The pan

A lot of cooks make the transition into the kitchen by putting on an apron. Me, I put my pan on the stove, bottom-right burner with the handle to the left, and, with that, I'm straight out of the traps and into dinner-land.

It's the little details that matter when it comes to getting the right pan. Get it right and it will be one of your most used items, but get it wrong and it's like sleeping in the wrong bed or driving the wrong car.

I've had successes and failures along the way and here's what I know.

I'd pick a sauté pan over a frying pan every day of the week. My sauté pan has deep, near vertical sides, rather than the typical slanted sides of a frying pan. This small design detail matters for several reasons. For a start, it's easier to stir-fry in without ingredients flying out. I find that slanted edges operate like all things slanted should – slides and ski-slopes, for example – by helping things to fly. Only that's not a particularly useful feature when cooking.

Pans, whether frying or sauté, are advertised based on their widest diameter, so my 11-inch sauté pan is just over 10 inches at the bottom, whereas my 11-inch frying pan is only 8 inches at the bottom. This might not sound like a big difference, but you'll really notice it when you're frying because with more space you can fry more in one go, like eggplant slices! Eggs! Mushrooms! More frying space means less time spent at the stove, less sweaty or steamed vegetables, and more time playing the spoons, or wherever you find your pleasure.

It's not only the base that's helpful here but the volume of food you can entertain. My 11-inch sauté pan, for example, holds almost 8 cups of liquid, while my 11-inch frying pan only holds about 6 cups. The extra volume gives the sauté pan more flexibility: I end up cooking curries in mine all the time.

I confess, I don't care if it's made of copper or old radiators; it's more important that it feels right in my hand. I want it to feel sturdy enough so that I can stir it without having to hold the handle the whole time (and I feel confident the food won't burn easily) but light enough to show it who's boss when I'm flipping and reversing, or just doing the washing-up.

Mine's a good-quality nonstick and can go into the oven, which are both great things. I tend to wipe mine out most of the time to keep it clean, but if it goes into the god of destruction of pans (the dishwasher) every now and then, it's okay.

Finally, buy pans with a lid. "Who uses a lid?" asked my friend Georgie, as I frantically swung my lids around the kitchen like Frisbees, trying to find the right one (I've since invested in a pan-lid rack). I do, all the time. Without a pan lid, the liquid in your pan will evaporate, which is great if you're frying or reducing sauces, but if you're steaming anything like rice or vegetables, you want to create a miniature sauna in the pan to allow the heat and liquid to penetrate your ingredients. It's a technique! It also reduces cooking time. Hello again, spoons.

Fungi
and the
family of
onions

Portobello mushroom pancakes with hoisin sauce

One day at the school gates, Mum collared my friend Wade Pang's mum, an excellent Chinese cook, and asked how she could make hoisin sauce at home. Mrs Pang introduced Mum to a canned sauce, and there began "The Time of Hoisin," where we ate the stuff on everything. It coincided with the time Dad accidentally bought mushroom compost instead of normal stuff, thereby giving us a truckload of mushrooms, and, well, a new star was born. Although you can still buy the canned sauce, it is tremendously sweet, and besides, it's much more satisfying to whip up this approximation in a matter of minutes.

NOTE You will need to source fermented black soybeans, labeled "salted black beans," for this recipe. You can find them in your local Chinese shop or online (p 310). You'll also need two large baking sheets — mine are around 16 x 12 inches.

SERVES 4

3 lbs (15 large) portobello mushrooms, *cut into ½-inch-thick slices*
5 tbsp toasted sesame oil
1 tbsp salted black beans
2 tsp Chinese five-spice powder
heaping ⅓ cup smooth peanut butter
3 tbsp brown rice or agave syrup
2½ tbsp rice vinegar
¼ cup light soy sauce
10 scallions
¾ English cucumber, *halved lengthways and seeded*
16 Chinese-style Peking duck pancakes
mayonnaise (vegan if you like), *to serve*

Preheat the oven to 425°F.

Put the sliced mushrooms into a large bowl, toss with the sesame oil, distribute evenly across two big baking sheets (there will be some overlap) and roast for 20 minutes.

Meanwhile, make the hoisin sauce. Place the salted black beans in a medium-sized bowl, add 5 teaspoons of water and mash well with a fork. Add the five-spice powder, peanut butter, syrup, vinegar and soy sauce and whisk to mix into a sauce. Leave to one side.

Cut the scallions in half, then shred into long, thin strips. Cut the cucumber into the same length and width as the scallions, then place both on a serving plate and cover with damp paper towel to keep them fresh.

When the mushrooms are ready, remove from the oven. Tip the baking sheets to collect any juices, spoon out and discard. Then put all the mushrooms on one baking sheet, pour over the hoisin sauce, toss to coat, and return to the oven for 10 minutes, so the sauce heats through and goes sticky. Meanwhile, warm the pancakes according to the package instructions.

To serve, spread a warm pancake with a little mayonnaise, top with mushrooms, a few slices of scallion and cucumber, roll up tight and eat.

VO/DF   PREP 10 mins / COOK 40 mins

Fungi and the family of onions

Shiitake rice with chilli pecan oil

A long time ago I worked at Tate Modern, where I learned about automatic drawing, in which an artist draws without thinking, with a view to exploring the subconscious. I'm not claiming to be an artist, but I do a lot of automatic cooking, where I haven't quite made a plan before cooking dinner. So this recipe might tell you about my deepest thoughts, or maybe just what was in my pantry.

NOTE   The pink pickled ginger, called *beni shoga* or *kizami shoga*, really lifts the finished dish, so it's worth finding. It's different from sushi ginger (which is sweeter and paler), although you could sub with that if you can't find the pink pickled stuff.

SERVES 4

½ oz dried shiitake mushrooms
1½ cups jasmine rice
canola oil
1 yellow onion, *finely sliced*
3 cloves of garlic, *crushed*
14 oz fresh mushrooms, *half wild (or mixed) and half chestnut, all finely sliced*
2 tbsp brown rice miso
2 tbsp light soy sauce
2 tbsp Shaoxing wine
salt
½ cup pecans, *finely chopped*
1 tbsp chipotle chilli flakes
4 scallions, *finely sliced*
1½ tbsp white wine vinegar
Japanese pink pickled ginger, *to serve*

Put the dried shiitake into a heatproof measuring pitcher and pour over 2 cups of freshly boiled water. Leave to soak for 10 minutes, then squeeze the mushrooms out into the pitcher. Top up the mushroom stock to 1¾ cups with tap water, if need be. Finely slice the mushrooms and put to one side. Wash the jasmine rice in a sieve, agitating it with your hand, until the water runs clear, then drain and set aside.

Heat 2½ tablespoons of oil in a wide, deep frying pan for which you have a lid and, when hot, add the onion and fry for 8 minutes, until soft. Add the garlic, fry for 3 minutes more, then add both the soaked and fresh mushrooms and cook for another 5 minutes or so, until the mushrooms have softened and reduced in volume. Stir in the miso and cook for 3 or 4 minutes, until the mushrooms start to catch and caramelize.

Add the rice to the pan, stir to coat the grains in the mushroom mixture, then pour in the mushroom stock, soy sauce, Shaoxing wine and ¼ teaspoon of salt. Stir again, bring to a boil, pop the lid on, turn down the heat to a simmer and cook for 15 minutes. After this time, turn off the heat but don't lift the lid, and leave to steam through for at least 5 minutes.

While the rice is cooking, make the pecan oil. Put the pecans, chilli flakes, scallions (reserve a tablespoon to garnish) and vinegar in a small saucepan with ⅓ cup of oil and ¾ teaspoon of salt. Briefly bring to a boil on a medium heat, then turn off the heat.

To serve, divide the rice between four plates, add a spoonful of pink pickled ginger and the reserved scallions, and drizzle with the pecan oil to taste.

Dinner at Shuko's

Shuko Oda's restaurant Koya, in Soho, is one of my and Hugh's favorite places to eat out. We love sitting knee to knee at the bar while the chefs quietly and conscientiously proffer up plate after bowl of simple, beautiful food. I like the *hiya-atsu*, or cold udon and hot broth dish, on which this recipe is based. There are three components to it: the broth, the cold noodles and a salted peanut miso, and with them you get a great interplay between the heat of the broth, the cold chewy noodles and the sweet, fatty saltiness from the miso.

NOTE Kombu is a type of dehydrated edible seaweed which makes a fantastic stock. It's available in East Asian supermarkets and online (p 310). You'll also need a blender for the peanut miso.

SERVES 4

1 cup salted peanuts

½ tbsp red miso

½ tbsp white miso

2½ tbsp oat or brown rice syrup

6 dried shiitake mushrooms

4- x 6-inch piece of kombu

2 x 1½ inches ginger (1½ oz),
  grated

4 x 5-oz portions of ready-to-cook
  udon noodles

5 oz fresh shiitake mushrooms,
  sliced, or whole if very small

⅓ sweetheart or napa cabbage
  (5 oz), *cut into ¾-inch wedges
  at the widest point*

2 tbsp light soy sauce

2 tbsp mirin

½ tsp salt

To make the salted peanut miso, pulverize the peanuts into powder in a blender, taking care not to turn them into peanut butter. Pour into a small bowl, add both the misos and the syrup and mix together really well. Roll into four balls and keep to one side.

To make the broth, place the dried mushrooms in a large pot. Make cuts in the kombu at 1½-inch intervals, but don't slice it up (so it's easy to remove later). Pour over 6 cups of boiling water and leave to soak for 15 minutes. Add the ginger to the pot, bring to a rolling boil, then strain the broth through a sieve, discard the mushrooms, ginger and kombu, and set the broth aside.

Bring a large pot of water to a boil, then add the udon noodles. Boil for 2 minutes, then drain, rinse with cold water until cold and leave to one side.

Put the broth back over the heat. Add the fresh mushrooms, cabbage, soy, mirin and salt, bring the pot back to a boil and take off the heat.

To serve, divide the noodles and peanut miso balls between four plates and ladle the broth into four bowls. To eat, sip a little of the broth, dip a noodle or two into the broth and chase it down with a piece of salted peanut miso, using the chopsticks to cut a little off at a time.

Fungi and the family of onions

Black bean and onion braised tofu

The ubiquity of Chinese takeaways in this country is a wonderful thing. They put black bean sauce on the map for a start. But unlike other dishes that have made it to our tables from afar, few people make black bean sauce at home. The key ingredient is salted fermented black beans, which although small have incredible heft with their fudgy texture and deeply funky and fruity dark chocolate flavor. Happily, they're easy to get a hold of (thanks also to ubiquitous Chinese supermarkets) and boast a ludicrous shelf life, meaning you can make your own sauce whenever, wherever and within minutes.

NOTE Fermented black beans, which are better known as "salted black beans," are easy to find in any Chinese supermarket; the most popular brand available here is Zheng Feng.

SERVES 4

¼ cup cornstarch
1¼ lbs extra-firm tofu, *drained*
canola oil
2 yellow onions, *cut into*
  ¾- x ¾-inch pieces, layers
  separated
2 red bell peppers, *cut into*
  ¾-inch cubes
1 tsp salt
1½ x ¾ inches ginger, *finely*
  chopped
4 cloves of garlic, *sliced wafer-thin*
¼ cup salted black beans, *rinsed*
  well, chopped
2 fresh red chillies, *sliced*
3 tbsp white wine vinegar
3 tbsp light soy sauce
cooked jasmine rice *(p 304),*
  to serve

In a small bowl, mix together 1½ tablespoons of cornstarch with ½ cup of water.

Tip the remaining 2½ tablespoons of cornstarch onto a shallow lipped plate. Pat the tofu dry with paper towel and cut into ¾-inch cubes, then toss with the cornstarch, using a spoon to make sure it coats all sides.

Put a large nonstick sauté pan over a medium heat, pour in 2 tablespoons of oil and, when it's hot, fry the tofu for 4 to 6 minutes on each side, until golden. Depending on the size of your pan, you might need to do this in two batches. Transfer the fried tofu to a plate and put to one side.

Put the same pan back over a medium to high heat, add 2 more tablespoons of oil and, when hot, add the onions, peppers and salt. Leave to fry and catch slightly in the oil, tossing every minute or so, for 6 minutes, or until the onions are just starting to blacken at the edges and soften. Add the ginger and garlic and fry for 2 minutes more, stirring occasionally, then add the black beans and sliced chillies. Stir to mix, then put the tofu back into the pan along with the cornstarch paste, vinegar and soy sauce. Simmer the sauce until reduced a little and toss to coat the tofu in the thickened sauce.

Transfer to a serving plate and serve with jasmine rice.

Crispy oyster mushroom skewers with bok choy salad

Oyster mushrooms are a strong all-rounder in the kitchen, seeming to straddle both plant and meat worlds in what they look and taste like when cooked. Here they're coated in a marinade my mother used to use when cooking Chinese food at home – honey, soy, garlic and ginger – and roasted until golden, crisp and juicy.

NOTE Make the rice first if you're eating it alongside. You'll need two large baking sheets (mine are 16 x 12 inches) and eight long metal or wooden skewers. If you're using wooden skewers, soak in water for 20 minutes beforehand.

MAKES 8 skewers, to serve 4

mushrooms
6 tbsp canola oil
3 tbsp liquid honey
3 tbsp light soy sauce
6 cloves of garlic, *crushed*
2 x 1½ inches ginger (1½ oz), *grated*
¼ tsp salt, *plus extra for the rice*
1¾ lbs oyster mushrooms

salad
8½ oz bok choy or choy sum
1 stalk of celery, *sliced into thin half-moons*
½ English cucumber, *sliced into thin half-moons*
2 tbsp toasted sesame oil, *plus extra to serve*
2 tbsp rice vinegar
2 tbsp light soy sauce
1 bird's-eye chilli, *finely chopped*
½ cup salted peanuts, *finely chopped*

mayo
¼ cup mayonnaise
1 tsp rice vinegar
¾ oz fresh chives, *finely chopped*

cooked jasmine rice *(p 304), to serve*

Preheat the oven to 425°F and line two large baking sheets with parchment paper.

To make the marinade for the mushrooms, put all the ingredients except for the mushrooms into a large mixing bowl and stir. Tear the larger mushrooms in half, keep the small ones intact and place all in the bowl with the marinade. Mix well with your hands until the mushrooms are coated.

Thread the mushrooms onto the skewers and place on the baking sheets. Bake for 20 minutes until golden brown and the edges are starting to catch. While the mushrooms are baking, prepare the salad and mayo.

Whether you're using bok choy or choy sum, cut the stems into ½-inch-thick slices and the leaves into 1-inch-thick slices. Put into a serving bowl along with the celery and cucumber. In a smaller bowl, make the dressing by combining the sesame oil, vinegar, soy sauce and chilli. Put the ingredients for the mayo into another small bowl and mix, leaving some chives to decorate the top.

Just before serving, whisk the dressing and toss through the salad. To serve, place the steamed rice in a shallow bowl, drizzle with sesame oil and sprinkle with salt. Put the skewers on a platter for people to help themselves, and serve alongside the salad and chive mayo, with the chopped peanuts sprinkled over the top.

DF PREP 10 mins / COOK 35 mins

Fungi and the family of onions

Celery and shiitake congee

This is one of my favorite "it's going to be okay" dishes. It's a recipe for the long days, the hard days and the days that don't go to plan.

NOTE Many white misos can appear brown, so to keep your miso congee cream-colored, look for a white "shiro" miso, also called "sweet white" miso.

SERVES 4

17½ oz head of celery
2 tbsp rice vinegar
6 tbsp mirin
¾ oz dried shiitake mushrooms
3 tbsp canola oil
1 yellow onion, *finely diced*
2 scallions, *whites and greens separated, finely sliced*
5 cloves of garlic, *crushed*
1½ tsp salt
¾ x ¾ inch ginger, *grated*
¾ cup jasmine rice
2 tbsp shiro or sweet white miso
2 tbsp light soy sauce
½ tbsp dark soy sauce
optional: store-bought fried onions, *to finish*

First prepare the celery pickle. Remove the base from the head of celery, then finely slice a third of the celery stalks and place them in a small bowl with the vinegar and 2 tablespoons of mirin, stir and put to one side. Chop the remaining celery stalks into ¼-inch dice and set aside.

Put the mushrooms into a heatproof measuring pitcher, pour over 3 cups of freshly boiled water and set aside while you prepare the congee. When the mushrooms are cool enough to handle, squeeze out any water back into the pitcher and put the mushrooms to one side.

To make the congee, put the oil into a large lidded pot over a medium heat and, when hot, add the onion, scallion whites, garlic and salt, and cook, stirring so it doesn't color, for 4 minutes. Add the diced celery and ginger, fry for 5 minutes, again stirring, then add the rice, miso, 2 tablespoons of mirin, 2½ cups of water, and all but the last tablespoon of mushroom stock in case there is any grit at the bottom of the pitcher. Bring to a boil, skimming off any scum, if you wish, then pop on a lid, cocked, and leave to simmer for 30 minutes.

While the congee is simmering, make the braised mushrooms. Slice the drained soaked mushrooms or leave whole if they're small, then put them into a small saucepan with the light and dark soy sauces and the remaining 2 tablespoons of mirin. Bring slowly to a boil on a low heat, then turn down to a simmer and cook for 10 minutes, until the liquid glazes the mushrooms and there's no liquid left at the bottom of the pan.

Ladle the congee into individual bowls, spoon over a quarter of the braised mushrooms, a little celery pickle, the reserved scallion greens and fried onions, if using, and serve hot.

Caramelized onion, saffron and potato pie

In every walk of life, there are unsung heroes. They're not necessarily timid, but they simply don't draw attention to themselves and the value they add or work they do. I would put onions, pastry, saffron and potatoes in this category. None tends to play a starring role, but, rather, vital supporting acts. In this recipe, however, I've given them a stage to shine on and they all come together in an act of magical alchemy.

NOTE You'll need an 8-inch springform cake pan for this recipe. If you're vegan, check the pastry is suitable for vegans. If you're vegetarian, you can use a beaten egg to brush the top of the pastry. I'd recommend a bowlful of salad leaves dressed with oil, Dijon mustard and lemon juice alongside.

SERVES 4

6 tbsp olive oil

3 large yellow onions (1½ lbs), *halved and thinly sliced*

2 tsp salt

5 cloves of garlic, *grated*

18 strands of saffron

¾ tsp coarsely ground black pepper

1½ tsp mild curry powder

2 x 9-inch unroll-and-bake frozen pie crusts, *vegan or all butter, thawed*

1½ lbs Yukon Gold potatoes, *peeled and cut into ⅛-inch-thick slices*

oat milk, or 1 egg, *beaten, for glazing*

Preheat the oven to 400°F and line an 8-inch springform cake pan with parchment paper.

Put the oil into a wide frying pan over a medium heat and, once hot, add the onions and salt and sauté, stirring regularly, for 20 minutes or more, until reduced and caramelized. Stir in the garlic, saffron, pepper and curry powder, cook for 3 minutes, then take off the heat.

Unroll the pastry and put the lined pan on top of one sheet. Using a table knife, score a circle in the pastry ¾ inch larger than the pan. Set aside.

Take the other sheet of pastry so the longest side is facing you, then cut an 3-inch strip off the right-hand side, leaving you with a square. Lay this square over the pan, gently push it down into the center, then press into the bottom and sides. Use the remaining strip to patch up the sides of the pan all the way up, allowing any excess to hang over the edge.

To fill the pie, take a third of the potato slices and layer them in the bottom of the pan, overlapping them by ¼ inch. Top with half the cooked onions, spreading them thinly over the potatoes, then add another layer of potatoes. Top this with the remaining onions and finish with a final layer of potatoes. It won't look like the pie is very full, but don't worry.

Remove the paper from the cut-out pastry circle, lay it on top of the final layer of potatoes and lightly press the edges inside the pan. Fold the overhanging edges back over the top and either crimp or seal them shut with a fork. Cut a ¾-inch cross in the middle of the lid. Cut out any decorative shapes you fancy from the leftover pastry and arrange on the top.

Brush the pastry lid all over with oat milk or beaten egg, then bake for 1 hour and 15 minutes or until there's no resistance when poked with a cake skewer. Remove the pie from the oven and leave to rest for 10 minutes.

To remove the pie, carefully run a palette knife all around the edge and, once the pan is cool, lift it up and over the top. Transfer to a serving plate, cut into thick wedges and serve warm with a bright, leafy salad.

Wild garlic and baby potato curry with lime pickle yogurt

If you want to find me between mid February and mid April, I'll be dancing around the fields like Julie Andrews, picking wild garlic to throw into my pot. It's like garlic but fresher, greener and more alive-tasting, and it makes a fantastic curry sauce to smother your newest potatoes in.

NOTE Wild garlic is best foraged (but can sometimes be found at farmers' markets). Look for it in early spring. This dish is best served straight away to keep the vibrant green color. If you eat it some time after making, the potatoes will suck up the sauce and you'll need to add a little water to loosen it.

SERVES 4

2 lbs baby white potatoes, *washed and cut into bite-size pieces*
5 oz wild garlic leaves, *washed and drained*
1¼ cups plain Greek yogurt
¼ cup canola oil
1 large yellow onion, *finely chopped*
¾ x ¾ inch ginger, *finely grated*
2 green finger (or serrano) chillies, *finely chopped*
1½ tsp ground cumin
½ tsp ground turmeric
1¾ tsp salt

lime pickle yogurt
¾ cup plain Greek yogurt
2 oz lime pickle
1 tbsp canola oil

naan *(p 306)* **and butter,** *to serve*

Place the potatoes in a large saucepan. Cover with cold water, cock a lid over the top and bring to a boil, then simmer for 10 minutes, or until tender and a knife slips easily through them, and drain.

In the meantime, make the lime pickle yogurt. Put the yogurt into a small serving bowl, then chop the lime pickle really finely and place over the top. Spoon over the oil without mixing and leave to one side.

Remove any thick stems from the wild garlic. Put a handful of leaves to one side. Roughly chop the rest and throw into a blender with 1¼ cups of Greek yogurt then blitz and leave to one side.

Put ¼ cup of oil into a large lidded frying pan over a medium heat and, when hot, add the onion. Fry for 10 minutes, until soft and turning golden, then add the ginger, chillies, cumin, turmeric and salt. Stir to mix, turn the heat down to low and fry for another 4 minutes, until the onions are very soft and reduced.

Still over a low heat, add the potatoes to the pan and stir-fry for a couple of minutes, then add the wild garlic and yogurt mixture, along with 7 tablespoons of water. Stir to mix, put the lid on and cook for 5 minutes. Remove the lid, lay the remaining whole garlic leaves over the top of the potatoes, cover again and cook for another 5 minutes, until wilted, then take off the heat.

Heat up the naan breads and generously butter them, then serve alongside the curry and lime pickle yogurt.

Oyster mushroom larb with sticky rice

For the uninitiated, larb is the national dish of Laos, but I first encountered it in Thailand. It's as refreshing as the first sip of an ice-cold Diet Coke on a searing hot day: the sweet, sour and hot dressing is so enlivening that, in an alternative world, it could be used intravenously to revive sick patients. Here it marries perfectly with the oyster mushrooms, which, after being given a golden crust in a hot pan, drink up the dressing as thirstily as I did.

NOTE Most major supermarkets sell fresh makrut lime leaves, but I like to buy mine in (cheaper) packages from the freezer aisle in my local Chinese supermarket. Vegan fish sauces vary in quality and taste (Tofuna makes a good one).

SERVES 2

1 cup sticky or glutinous rice

4 large shallots (5 oz net), *sliced into wafer-thin rings*

6 makrut lime leaves, *deveined and thinly sliced*

2 bird's-eye chillies, *finely chopped*

1 tbsp soft light brown sugar

3 tbsp lime juice, *from 2–3 limes*

2½ tbsp vegan fish sauce

½ tsp salt

14 oz oyster mushrooms

canola oil

½ oz fresh mint leaves, *chopped*

½ oz fresh cilantro leaves, *chopped*

1 romaine lettuce, *trimmed, leaves separated*

2½ tbsp salted peanuts, *crushed to a powder with a pestle and mortar or very finely chopped*

Tip the rice into a sieve and rinse under the cold tap until the water runs clear. Cover the rice with hand-hot water and leave to soak for 30 minutes.

Meanwhile, make the larb dressing. Put the shallots, lime leaves, chillies, sugar, lime juice and vegan fish sauce into a medium-sized mixing bowl, stir to mix and leave to one side.

Drain the rice, put it in a pot, cover with 1¼ cups of water, add the salt and put the lid on. Bring to a boil, then turn down the heat to its lowest setting and simmer for 15 minutes, until all the water has evaporated and the rice is cooked. Leave to stand for at least 10 minutes, without lifting the lid.

While the rice is cooking, tear the mushrooms into ¾-inch-wide lengths. Heat a tablespoon of oil in a large nonstick frying pan over a medium to high heat and, when burning hot, add half the mushrooms. Cook for 4 to 5 minutes, turning once or twice at most to get a lovely golden sear on them. Scrape into the bowl with the dressing, add more oil to the pan and fry the second batch. Add to the same bowl, then fold through the mint and cilantro.

To serve, either keep in the bowl or tip the mushrooms onto a lipped plate. To eat, take a lettuce leaf, spoon in a heaping tablespoon of sticky rice and top with a heaping tablespoon of larb, making sure you get plenty of dressing. Sprinkle with crushed peanuts, fold closed and eat straight away.

Pictured overleaf

A

pocketful

of

pulses

Iraqi white bean stew

This is one of the most popular recipes from my column. I wrote it after speaking to my friend Assallah's mum, Amina, about her *fasoulia*, or white bean stew. I tend to cook it when I'm staying with friends because it's a ludicrously easy dish to cook away from home (just pack the cans and spices), or at Christmas time when there are a lot of people in the house to feed, and the smell of the spices and the warmth of a big pot of beans gently simmering away happily fill the kitchen.

NOTE Amina uses a pre-bought Iraqi seven-spice mix called *baharat* in her recipe, which you could use instead of the spices in mine. This recipe doubles easily. Make the rice first if you're eating it alongside.

SERVES 4

canola oil, *for frying*
2 yellow onions, *finely chopped*
salt
½ tsp ground black pepper
½ tsp ground cinnamon
1 tsp ground allspice
½ tsp ground cumin
1¾ oz fresh cilantro, *leaves and stems finely chopped*
1 x 14-oz can of chopped tomatoes
2 x 15-oz cans of cannellini beans, *drained*
1 lemon, *zested, and juiced to get 3 tbsp*

cooked basmati rice *(p 305), to serve*

Put 3 tablespoons of oil into a large, heavy-bottomed saucepan on a medium heat. Once hot, add the onions, a teaspoon of salt, the black pepper, cinnamon, allspice, cumin and cilantro stems, and cook, stirring occasionally, for 20 minutes, until soft and dark. Keep an eye on it, because you don't want the onions or spices to catch.

When the mix is soft and sweet-smelling, add the tomatoes, beans and half a can of water, bring up to a boil, then simmer for 10 minutes.

To make the lemon and cilantro oil, place ¼ cup of oil in a bowl and add the cilantro leaves, lemon zest and juice, and ¼ teaspoon of salt. Mix and leave to one side.

Transfer the stew to a large serving bowl and top with the lemon and cilantro oil. Serve with rice alongside and allow people to help themselves.

V / GF   PREP 10 mins / COOK 35 mins

A pocketful of pulses

Fennel and dill dal

Of course dals are great in autumn and winter, but they're also good all year round. This one is warming but it has a freshness to it from the dill and lime that just feels right on a summer's evening. I first ate it when it was delivered to my door by the London-based tiffin delivery service DabbaDrop. Anshu Ahuja from DabbaDrop was kind enough to send me her recipe, which I have lightly adapted here.

NOTE You'll need the yellow split insides of mung beans, called "mung dal," which can be found in South Asian supermarkets and online (p 310). Make the rice first if you're eating it alongside.

SERVES 4

1½ cups yellow split mung dal
1 tsp ground turmeric
1¼ tsp salt
¼ cup canola oil
1 tsp cumin seeds
1½ tsp black mustard seeds
1 yellow onion, *finely chopped*
1 large fennel bulb, *finely chopped*
¾ oz fresh dill, *leaves roughly chopped*
2 green finger (or serrano) chillies, *finely chopped*
4 cloves of garlic, *crushed*
½ x 14-oz can of coconut milk
1½ tbsp lime juice, *from 1 lime*

cooked basmati rice *(p 305)* or chapattis *(p 307), to serve*

Rinse the mung dal in a sieve under the cold tap until the water runs clear, put into a large pot with the turmeric and cover with 5 cups of water. Bring to a boil, turn down the heat and simmer for 20 to 25 minutes, until cooked — that is, when the lentils start to break down and merge together when stirred. Stir in the salt and set aside.

While the lentils are cooking, put the oil into a large frying pan over a medium heat and, once it's properly hot (test by placing a wooden spoon in the pan: it's ready when the oil bubbles around it), add the cumin and mustard seeds. Thirty seconds later, when they pop, add the onion, fennel and half the chopped dill, and cook, stirring every now and then, until soft and caramelized, which should take about 20 minutes.

Reserve a couple of tablespoons of the fennel and onion mixture to decorate the final dish. Add the chillies and garlic to the remaining fennel mixture, stir-fry for 3 minutes more, then tip into the lentil pot along with the coconut milk; if the mixture looks as if it could do with being a bit looser, add a little water. Bring the mix up to a bubble, then take off the heat and stir through the lime juice. Taste and adjust the salt, lime and/or chilli as you wish.

To serve, ladle the dal over the rice, if using, and scatter over the remaining fennel and onion and chopped dill.

No-cook salad with tomatoes, chickpeas and rose harissa

The perfect assembly job. For when it's too hot to cook but you still want to eat something delicious.

NOTE Jarred chickpeas are fantastic for salads, because they are ludicrously creamy. If you have only canned, use two cans and to get rid of any chalkiness, put the chickpeas and their water into a saucepan, bring to a boil and simmer for 5 minutes, then drain, to get super-soft chickpeas. Belazu makes an incomparable rose harissa.

SERVES 2

dressing

3 tbsp rose harissa paste
3 tbsp extra virgin olive oil
3 tbsp lemon juice, *from 1–2 lemons*
1 tsp salt

salad

1 x 24-oz jar of cooked chickpeas
½ red onion, *finely sliced*
30 baby plum tomatoes (10 oz), *halved*
1 English cucumber (12 oz), *seeded and cut into ½-inch half-moons*
20 pitted Kalamata olives, *halved*
¾ oz fresh cilantro
¾ oz fresh mint, *leaves picked*

pita bread or flatbreads
(pp 305–6), to serve

Put all the dressing ingredients into a bowl and stir. Drain the chickpeas, tip into a large bowl, and add the onion, tomatoes, cucumber and olives. Pour the dressing over the vegetables and mix well. Finely chop the cilantro, and all but a small handful of mint leaves. Sprinkle over the chopped cilantro and mint, and fold through the salad.

To serve, toast the pita breads or heat the flatbreads and cut into pieces. Tip the salad out onto a serving platter, scatter over the remaining mint leaves and serve with the bread on the side.

A pocketful of pulses

Borlotti beans, chopped salad and tahini

I first ate *ful medames*, the dish on which this recipe is based, at Gaby's, a Jewish deli on Charing Cross Road in London. For the uninitiated, it's a thick stew made using dried fava beans, spiced with cumin and garlic and brightened with lemon and herbs. They're the sort of beans that would make you feel at home anywhere. Sadly, Gaby's has since closed and dried fava beans are hard to come by, so here's a quicker version using canned borlotti. It's not quite the same (both the dish and without Gaby's), but it is just as homely.

SERVES 2

salad

½ **English cucumber,** *cut into ¼-inch slices*

2 **medium tomatoes,** *cut into ½-inch-thick wedges*

¼ **red onion,** *finely diced*

5 **tbsp lemon juice,** *from 2 lemons*

salt

beans and tahini

3 **tbsp extra virgin olive oil,** *plus extra to serve*

2 **cloves of garlic,** *finely sliced*

2 **tsp ground cumin**

½ **tsp ground black pepper**

½ **tsp ground cinnamon**

2 **medium-sized ripe tomatoes,** *roughly chopped*

2 x 15-oz **cans of borlotti (cranberry) beans,** *drained*

3 **tbsp tahini**

to serve

cracked black pepper

warmed flatbreads *(pp 305–6)* or pita bread

Make the chopped salad first, to give it time to marinate. Put the cucumber, tomatoes and red onion into a bowl with 3 tablespoons of the lemon juice and ¼ teaspoon of salt, toss to combine and set aside.

Warm 2 tablespoons of oil in a frying pan on a medium heat and, once hot, gently fry the garlic for 2 minutes, just until it begins to color. Stir in the spices, leave them to sizzle for a minute, then add the tomatoes and ½ teaspoon of salt. Cook for 3 minutes, breaking the tomatoes down with a wooden spoon, then add the beans and half a can of water. Bring to a boil, then turn down the heat to a simmer and leave to cook for 15 minutes, crushing some of the beans a little to thicken the mixture.

While the beans are cooking, make the tahini dressing. Put the tahini into a bowl and whisk in the remaining 2 tablespoons of lemon juice and ¼ teaspoon of salt – it will split at first, but don't worry, it will come back together later. Add a tablespoon of oil and 2 tablespoons of water, and whisk again until you have a smooth sauce.

Serve the beans either in the pan or in two shallow bowls, drizzled with more olive oil and some freshly cracked pepper, alongside the chopped salad, tahini sauce and warmed flatbreads or pita bread.

Lima beans in salsa verde

Hannah, my recipe tester, never lets her emotions get in the way of her professional recipe feedback and has largely kept a poker face in the decade that we've worked together (except for the time she kicked a beet dessert into the trash). This recipe, however, came back with a note: "The whole family is *obsessed!!!*" And, I thought, "This is as close to the stars as I'll ever fly."

NOTE For a bit of texture, and stress relief, finely chop the herbs to mince them, or else use a food processor or blender.

SERVES 2

¾ oz fresh flat-leaf parsley

¾ oz fresh basil leaves

¾ oz fresh mint, *leaves picked*

3 tbsp brined capers, *drained*

2 cloves of garlic, *finely sliced*

1 tbsp red wine vinegar

5 tbsp extra virgin olive oil, *plus 2 tbsp for the beans*

2 x 15-oz cans of lima beans in water, *not drained*

1 yellow onion, *finely chopped*

optional: 1 red chilli, *finely chopped*

¾ tsp salt, *or to taste*

warmed flatbreads *(pp 305–6)* or toasted ciabatta, *to serve*

To make the salsa verde, put all the herbs on a large chopping board and finely chop with the capers and one of the sliced garlic cloves, then transfer to a bowl, stir in the vinegar and the oil, and put to one side (alternatively, put all these ingredients into the small bowl of a food processor and pulse until chopped and mixed).

Drain away about 3 tablespoons of the liquid from one of the cans of lima beans, but leave the other one as it is. Put 2 tablespoons of oil into a large frying pan over a medium heat and, once hot, add the onion and cook, stirring occasionally, for 8 minutes, until really soft and starting to turn golden. Add the second sliced garlic clove and the chilli, cook, stirring, for a couple of minutes, then tip in the lima beans and all their remaining liquid. Simmer for about 10 minutes, until the beans are soft and the stock has reduced a little, then stir in the salsa verde and salt to taste. Take off the heat and serve at once with warmed flatbreads or toasted ciabatta to mop up the juices.

V/GFO (WITH GF BREAD) PREP 10 mins / COOK 20 mins

A pocketful of pulses

Lentil soup with harissa and preserved lemon

Straight out of the family cookbook, here is a soup I made for Hugh when he was run-down and watching endless sports documentaries in bed. I wanted to make him something brothy and invigorating but wholesome and satisfying too – and this was the result. The preserved lemon, harissa and mint really make it, so skip those at your peril. Chuck whichever greens you like in, though – just be sure to cook them until they're soft.

NOTE A spoonful of plain Greek yogurt and some store-bought fried onions make unnecessary but advisable additions.

SERVES 4

3½ tbsp extra virgin olive oil, *plus extra to serve*

1 large yellow onion, *finely chopped*

2 stalks of celery, *finely chopped*

4 cloves of garlic, *crushed*

1–2 preserved lemons (1¾ oz), *seeded and finely chopped*

1 tbsp harissa paste

1 cup dried green lentils

6 cups vegetable stock

½ tsp salt

7 oz broccolini, *chopped into ½-inch pieces*

7 oz Swiss chard, *stalks and leaves shredded*

½ oz fresh mint leaves, *chopped*

optional: plain Greek or dairy-free yogurt, *and* store-bought fried onions, *to serve*

Put the oil into a large pot over a medium heat. When hot, add the onion and celery and cook for 12 minutes, or until soft, golden and threatening to brown. Add the garlic, lemon and harissa and cook for 5 minutes, stirring. Add the lentils, stock and salt, and bring to a boil, then turn the heat down and leave to blip and bubble for 20 minutes. Add the greens and more hot water if need be (I add an extra 1¼ cups) and cook for a final 10 minutes, or until the lentils are tender and the greens are soft and emerald. Take off the heat and stir through half the mint.

To serve, divide between your bowls, top with yogurt and fried onions (if you wish) and the remaining mint, then drizzle generously with extra virgin olive oil.

Malaysian dal curry

This is the first recipe I wrote down in the battered orange notebook. It's based on a Malaysian-style dal curry we ate gallons of on a trip to Singapore. It's more fragrant than Indian dal, it has more aromatics such as lemongrass and star anise, and it's as soothing to cook (all in one pot) as it is to eat, because the coconut milk softens the edges somewhat.

NOTE This should be a cheap meal, especially if you buy the ingredients from an Asian supermarket. Serve with paratha (buy them from the freezer section of your local Asian supermarket or make the quick one on p 190), or steamed basmati rice.

SERVES 4

3 tbsp canola oil
10 fresh curry leaves
1 stalk of lemongrass, *bruised*
2 star anise
1 yellow onion, *finely chopped*
2 cloves of garlic, *crushed*
1 tsp ground coriander
1 tsp ground cumin
½ tsp ground turmeric
1½ tsp Kashmiri chilli powder
1½ tbsp tomato paste
1½ cups red lentils
1¼ tsp salt
2 medium carrots (5 oz), *peeled and cut into ½-inch cubes*
1 x 14-oz can of coconut milk
1 tbsp tamarind paste, *or to taste*

to serve
chilli crisp
paratha, naan *(p 306)* or
  cooked basmati rice *(p 305)*

Put the oil into a large saucepan on a medium heat and, once hot, add the curry leaves, lemongrass and star anise and cook until the leaves crackle. Stir in the onion, cook for about 8 minutes, until soft and translucent, then add the garlic and cook for 2 minutes more.

Add the coriander, cumin, turmeric and chilli powder, stir to mix, then add the tomato paste, lentils and salt, and cook for 2 minutes.

Add the carrots and coconut milk, then fill up the empty coconut milk can twice with tap water and add that to the pan, too. Cook, stirring occasionally, for about 20 to 25 minutes, until the dal is nice and thick and the carrots tender. Stir through a tablespoon of tamarind paste, then taste and adjust the tamarind, adding more, teaspoon by teaspoon, until it tastes just right to you. Serve in bowls topped with a spoonful of chilli crisp and alongside the paratha, naan or basmati rice.

V/GFO   PREP 5 mins / COOK 35 mins

Cheesy masala beans on toast

Not long after my parents were married, they lived in a council flat in Scunthorpe. With very little money, they had to cook thriftily, which led to them eating these curried baked beans on toast as a regular midweek meal. To this day it stands the test of time as a great, delicious and inexpensive dish.

NOTE When this recipe was published in the *Guardian*, I served it with cilantro chutney – but at home, we sometimes like to grate cheese over the top instead. If you'd like to keep it vegan, remove the cheese and make the cilantro chutney on p 308.

SERVES 2

beans
2 tbsp canola oil
1 **red onion,** *finely chopped*
2 **cloves of garlic,** *crushed*
1 **green finger (or serrano) chilli,**
    finely chopped
1 **heaping tsp tomato paste**
1 **tsp ground coriander**
½ **tsp ground turmeric**
½ **tsp ground cumin**
¼ **tsp salt**
1 x 15-oz **can of baked beans**

to serve
2 **large or 3 small slices of**
    sourdough bread
unsalted butter, *vegan or dairy*
4 oz **sharp Cheddar,** *grated*
½ **green finger (or serrano) chilli,**
    finely sliced

To cook the beans, heat the oil in a frying pan and, once hot, add all except for 2 tablespoons of the onion (leave this to one side). Cook, stirring regularly, for 8 minutes, until soft, golden and translucent. Add the garlic and chilli, cook, stirring, for 2 minutes more, then add the tomato paste, all the spices and the salt. Cook for 1 minute, then add the beans and cook for a couple of minutes, adding a tablespoon or two of water if it's looking a little dry. Take off the heat.

Heat the broiler and place the bread on a baking sheet. When hot, place under the broiler for 2 minutes, then remove, flip over and generously butter the bread, and broil for another minute or so. Top with the beans, then sprinkle over the Cheddar, reserved onion and green chilli. Broil for another 6 minutes, until the cheese is golden and molten, and serve straight away.

Gujarati mung bean dal with sambharo

Mung beans are considered very lucky to the average Gujarati. Uncooked, they're popular at religious ceremonies – I still have a pocketful that was blessed at my wedding. Today, they are just here as an idea for dinner – which you won't need any luck to make. This is a simple and gentle dal, but it does need a perky sidekick, hence the sambharo, a sweet-and-sour cabbage-and-carrot relish, alongside.

NOTE You'll need fresh curry leaves, which can be found in larger supermarkets or in Indian supermarkets. Freeze any you don't use for next time.

SERVES 4

dal
2 tbsp canola oil
½ tsp cumin seeds
1 tsp black mustard seeds
1¾ cups passata or crushed canned
    tomatoes
1 x ¾ inch ginger, *finely grated*
1 green finger (or serrano) chilli,
    finely chopped
1 tsp ground coriander
1 tsp ground cumin
1¼ tsp salt
2 cups whole mung beans

sambharo
2 tbsp canola oil
1 tsp black mustard seeds
2 green finger (or serrano) chillies,
    slit lengthways
6 fresh curry leaves
¼ green cabbage (7 oz), *finely
    shredded*
2 carrots (7 oz), *peeled with
    a julienne peeler or grated*
¾ tsp salt
1½ tsp lemon juice
¼ tsp superfine sugar

to serve
chapattis *(p 307)* **or cooked**
    basmati rice *(p 305)*
plain Greek or dairy-free yogurt

Put the oil into a large saucepan over a medium heat and, when hot, add the cumin seeds and mustard seeds, and leave to pop for 20 to 30 seconds. Turn the heat right down and gently add the tomatoes to the pan— watch out, the oil might spit. Crank the heat back up to medium, then cook, stirring, for 5 minutes, until the tomatoes bubble thickly. Stir in the ginger, chilli, coriander, ground cumin and salt, cook for 2 minutes more, then add the mung beans and 5 cups of water. Bring to a boil, then turn down to a whisper and cook, stirring every now and then, for 45 minutes, until the beans are soft (but not mushy) and you can squash them easily against the side of the pan.

While the dal is cooking, make the sambharo. Heat the oil in a frying pan and, when hot, add the mustard seeds, chillies and curry leaves, and let them crackle and pop for 30 seconds. Add the cabbage and carrot, stir-fry for 5 minutes, until the vegetables have wilted but still have some crunch, then add the salt, lemon juice and sugar. Take off the heat, taste and adjust the seasoning accordingly.

Serve the dal alongside chapattis or rice, with the sambharo and some yogurt on the side.

VO/GF0   PREP 10 mins / COOK 1 hr

Sunday kitchari

Kitchari is traditionally what the women in my family would cook when they were tired or convalescing–but there's Deliveroo for that now. So this is a slightly embellished variation of an everyday meal made from a mixture of rice and lentils. I like to make it on a Sunday when I want to cook and would like some comfort food, but I want the oven to do most of the hard work.

NOTE There are two types of kitchari: wet and dry. I prefer mine more like rice than risotto, but feel free to add more water. You'll need a casserole dish suitable for the oven and stove for which you have a lid. Mung dal is the dehusked yellow split lentil of the whole green mung bean; it's available in South Asian supermarkets and online (p 310).

SERVES 4

1 cup basmati rice

1 cup mung dal

3 tbsp canola oil

1 tsp cumin seeds

1 yellow onion, *finely chopped*

a large handful (1¾ oz) of roasted unsalted cashews

¾ x ¾ inch ginger, *finely chopped*

2 medium tomatoes (5 oz), *chopped*

2 green finger (or serrano) chillies, *finely chopped*

1 tsp ground turmeric

1¾ tsp salt

to serve

plain Greek or dairy-free yogurt

lime pickle or other Indian pickles

a handful of fresh cilantro, *finely chopped*

1 lemon, *cut into wedges*

Preheat the oven to 425°F.

Put the rice and mung dal into a bowl and cover with cold water, agitate them with your hand, then drain and repeat until the water is clear. Drain again, then place in a bowl, cover with fresh cold water and leave to soak while you prepare the other ingredients.

Put the oil into a casserole pot over a medium to high heat. When hot, add the cumin seeds, let them sizzle for 30 seconds, then add the onion and cashews. Cook for 6 to 8 minutes, until the onion starts to bronze around the edges, then add the ginger, tomatoes, chillies, turmeric and salt. Cook for 3 minutes, then add the rice and lentils and mix together. Add 3 cups of water, pop the lid on and place in the center of the oven for 30 minutes. Remove from the oven, but leave the lid on for a further 10 minutes.

To serve, pile into bowls, dollop over the yogurt, add a spoonful of your favorite pickle, scatter over the cilantro and place a lemon wedge alongside.

Tupperware

Thanks to my parents' immigrant mindset, my childhood was nothing if not thrifty. Everything that could be recycled was done, many times over. Top of the list were presents. Many arrived in boxes patchy from where the Sellotape had been ripped off, already having done the rounds in the Indian community. They went straight into "the present cupboard," in which also lived small Wedgwood rabbits, cut-glass bowls and potpourri waiting to find new homes where they could finally be loved.

Second on the list: plastic food containers.

I could tell just from the sound of the click of the seal what was being opened for dinner. The Carte d'Or tubs had the loudest, most reassuring click, and were the only ones Mum would trust to store curries and dals. The soft click of the ancient 1980s Vitalite tub, which housed chapatti flour, denoted it was time to make the daily roti, while the jolly chirp of the Lancashire Farm bucket meant that it was "nasto" time (snack time): always home-made Bombay mix.

When I set up my own kitchen in my new home, I endeavored to follow in Mum's footsteps and build my own reused plastic food-container collection. For a couple of years, I succeeded with a pile of warped, turmeric-stained ones, complete with miscellaneous lids that would come crashing out of the cupboard every time I opened it: I was keeping my dream of being a good Indian daughter alive.

Then, one day, without warning and while in a certain Swedish furniture giant, I fell, lid over tub, for the ultimate food container, the IKEA 365+. A cold sweat passed over me. Could I break away from Mum and the Indian community and challenge decades of Indian orthodoxy?

I did, and I can credit my new food-storage system for having made my life easier, my fridge neater, my marriage smoother and my food, well, more accessible.

What makes good food containers great?

For a start, this particular container is glass, meaning you can see, at a glance, what's inside and what possibilities lie ahead for dinner, without an olfactory dance around the fridge. This might not make me faster or more efficient, but it does make me happier.

With glass, you can also go from the fridge to the microwave, oven or even the freezer in one swift movement. As an added bonus, glass won't stain or hold smells like plastic does, it's better for the environment and it can go in the dishwasher.

Unless you're blessed with a large kitchen and ample storage, stackability is important and so a system is key. The IKEA 365+ containers have sloping sides, so that they can neatly fold into one another like wedding chairs in a town hall, in your cupboard.

Whichever system you go for, try and find one that has the same lid for all containers, no matter the volume. This is a small mercy if you've ever lost hours of your life (like I had) trying to find the right one.

Size matters in the kitchen. The 34-oz container will generally hold enough food for four (depending on what it is, but let's say dal or rice), while the more voluptuous 61-ounce I tend to use for batch cooking, or proofing pizza dough.

Of course, no great food-storage life can exist without the all-important accoutrements: masking tape and a Sharpie to label and date your food with. My sister recently cooked dinner for us, defrosting some apple-and-berry crumble for dessert, only to realize that it was, in fact, borscht.

And my parting advice to you would be this. There are two types of people in this world: those who "get" good food containers and those who don't. Unless you're sure which type you're dealing with, never ever lend it out. I'm still not on speaking terms with Jen at number 38 after having made the wrong call.

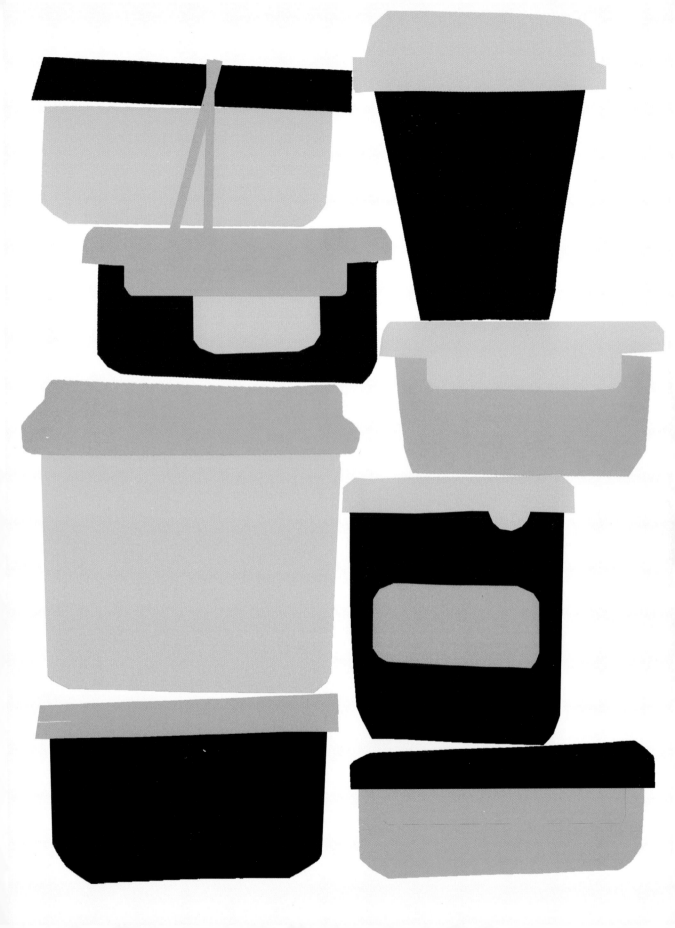

Roots, shoots and tubers

18-carat laksa

The only thing I know of to be more successful than this recipe in dispatching a whole bag of carrots is a horse. Roasted, the carrots' natural sweetness counters the intensity of the aromatics and spices in this curried laksa and, along with the coconut milk, balances it out perfectly. On a separate note, it's taken me ten years to finally write a recipe that uses 2 pounds of carrots for a main course. I'm so proud of it, I may just frame it and put it up next to my Grade 1 piano certificate in the downstairs bathroom.

NOTE Most of the ingredients in this recipe go straight into a blender to create the laksa paste. You can buy tofu puffs in Chinese supermarkets and online (p 310). Laksa noodles (medium rice vermicelli) are difficult to source; when I can't find them, I use wheat ramen noodles or rice sticks instead.

SERVES 4

quick pickled bean sprouts
3½ oz bean sprouts
2 tbsp white wine vinegar
2 tsp salt

laksa
2 lbs carrots, *peeled*
2 tbsp + 6 tbsp canola oil
salt
1 yellow onion, *chopped*
6 cloves of garlic, *chopped*
1 x 1 inch ginger, *chopped*
2 stalks of lemongrass, *outer leaves and top third discarded, the rest chopped*
15 fresh curry leaves
4 tsp Kashmiri chilli powder
2 tsp mild curry powder
1 tbsp superfine sugar
2½ tbsp light soy sauce
1 x 14-oz can of coconut milk
8 oz or 16 tofu puffs
11 oz medium rice vermicelli noodles
¾ oz fresh Thai basil, *leaves picked, to serve*

Preheat the oven to 425°F.

To make the pickle, pop the bean sprouts into a small heatproof bowl with the vinegar, salt and ⅔ cup of freshly boiled water and leave to one side for 10 minutes, then drain.

Meanwhile, halve the carrots lengthways and chop into 1-inch chunks. Place in a single layer on a large roasting pan or two, drizzle over 2 tablespoons of oil and sprinkle over ½ teaspoon of salt. Mix with your hands and roast for 40 minutes.

While the carrots are roasting, make the laksa paste. Place 6 tablespoons of oil in a small blender along with the onion, garlic, ginger, lemongrass, curry leaves, 1¼ teaspoons of salt, the chilli powder, curry powder and sugar and blend to a smooth paste. Scrape every last bit of the paste into a large pot, then rinse out the blender and keep to one side – you'll need to use it again. Heat the paste in a large saucepan or pot over a medium heat for 12 minutes, stirring regularly, then add the soy sauce, coconut milk, roasted carrots, tofu puffs and 3½ cups of water.

Bring to a boil and simmer for 8 minutes, then take a heaping ladleful of the carrots with some of the liquid and pop it into the blender. Blitz until smooth, then add back to the pot and stir. Turn the heat off and pop a lid on, while you cook the noodles according to the package instructions.

To serve, distribute the noodles across four bowls, then ladle the laksa and carrots between the bowls. Place a small pile of pickled bean sprouts on top, along with a few Thai basil leaves.

Roots, shoots and tubers

Sweet potato summer rolls

No one knows their way around rice or rolls better than the Vietnamese. The fact that rice papers exist, the dried sheets that transform into a thin, silky wrapper, is a feat of incredible human innovation and ingenuity.

NOTE   These make for a light summer meal. Summer rolls are a bit like pancakes: the first one is always rubbish and you get the hang of them as you go along. Not all vegan fish sauces are equal (Tofuna makes a good one); use the best-quality one you can find.

MAKES 16, to serve 4

summer rolls
4 sweet potatoes (1½ lbs)
2 tbsp canola oil
2 tbsp teriyaki marinade
5 oz rice vermicelli noodles
½ cup crunchy peanut butter
1 oz fresh mint, *leaves picked*
1 oz fresh cilantro, *leaves picked*
3½ oz baby-leaf spinach
16 rice paper rolls, 8½ inches in
    diameter

dipping sauce
2 cloves of garlic, *crushed*
1 tbsp superfine sugar
2 bird's-eye chillies, *finely chopped*
2 tbsp vegan fish sauce
1½ tbsp lime juice, *from 1 lime*

Preheat the oven to 425°F.

Wash the sweet potatoes and cut lengthways into ¼-inch slices (no need to peel them). Place them in a bowl and pour over the oil and teriyaki marinade, then rub to coat them and tip onto two large baking sheets. Bake for 20 minutes, or until golden and blackening in spots.

Meanwhile, put all the ingredients for the dipping sauce into a small bowl with 2 tablespoons of water and mix. Split into two small bowls for easy access, or even four (double the recipe if need be), and leave to one side. Prepare the noodles according to the package instructions, then drain, rinse under cold water and drain again. Snip with a pair of kitchen scissors to make them easier to handle and then leave to one side.

Once the sweet potato slices are out of the oven, prepare a rolling station. You'll need a large chopping board, a large bowl of hand-hot water to dip the papers in, and the filling ingredients – the peanut butter, herbs, spinach, sweet potato slices and noodles.

Dip one rice paper into the water, rotating it like a wheel to get it wet. Be brave and brief – it should still be firm-ish – and pop it onto your chopping board. Place two sweet potato slices on the lower third of the paper, then dollop on a heaping teaspoon of peanut butter and spread it over the potato with the back of the spoon. Top with a big pinch of spinach (around 10 leaves), then a big pinch of noodles (around 1 oz) and roll once. Place a few mint leaves and cilantro leaves on the paper, next to the rolled bit, then roll again, folding in the sides. Put it to one side and repeat. You may need to top up your soaking water with hot water from the kettle, as you go along.

These are best eaten shortly after they're made, but you can keep them fresh by putting a clean, damp kitchen towel over them. Serve on a large platter with the bowls of dipping sauce alongside.

Hasselback celery root with miso and red onion salad

Inspiration for a new dish can strike from anywhere. In this case, I loved the sound of "hasselback celery root" so much that I had to create a recipe just for the name – but now I don't think I'll ever be able to eat it un-hasselbacked again. Cutting deep fans into the celery root means there's more surface area to roast and to spread miso over, creating richer and deeper flavors, while the tops catch in the heat and crisp to a satisfying crunch.

NOTE Don't be put off by the cooking time: the oven does most of the work, and the sauce and salad come together in minutes.

SERVES 4

celery root
1 large or 2 small celery root
   (2 to 2½ lbs total)
3–4 tbsp olive oil
salt
⅓ cup shiro or sweet white miso
½ tbsp Aleppo pepper
2½ tbsp brown rice or agave syrup
1½ tbsp lemon juice, *from 1 lemon*

tahini sauce
½ cup tahini
1 tbsp lemon juice, *from ½ lemon*
½ tsp salt

red onion salad
1 red onion, *halved and thinly sliced*
1 tbsp pomegranate molasses
1 tbsp lemon juice
1 tsp ground sumac
3 tbsp olive oil
¼ tsp salt
a large handful of fresh flat-leaf
   parsley, *leaves picked, plus more*
   to serve

flatbreads *(pp 305–6), to serve*

Preheat the oven to 400°F. Trim the base and peel the skin of the celery root using a potato peeler. Use the tip of a knife to hoick out any muddy crevices. If the celery root is large, cut it in half (if not, leave it), then cut across the celery root in ¼-inch intervals down to ¾ inch from the base, and stop cutting.

Drizzle oil between the folds, rub more oil all over the top, and sprinkle with salt. Place on a nonstick baking sheet, roast for 45 minutes, remove and, if need be, baste with more oil. Return to the oven for another 45 minutes, until golden and a knife slides into the bottom without any resistance.

While the celery root is cooking, make the accompaniments. To make the miso glaze, mix the miso, Aleppo pepper, syrup and lemon juice in a small bowl and set to one side.

Put all the ingredients for the tahini sauce into a small serving bowl, whisk with 5 tablespoons of water and set to one side.

Combine all the salad ingredients in a serving bowl, scrunch together with your (clean) hands, to wilt the onions a little, and set to one side.

Once the celery root is done, remove the baking sheet from the oven, carefully brush the celery root all over with the glaze – you want it to stay on the celery root, not slip off – making sure it gets between the slits, then bake for a final 15 minutes.

To serve, warm the flatbreads. Take the whole celery root, red onion salad, tahini sauce, flatbreads and some parsley leaves to the table. Encourage people to assemble their own plates, with a smoosh of tahini on the bread, followed by a few slices of celery root and a tangle of the onion salad and parsley.

V/GFO (WITH GF BREAD)   PREP 10 mins / COOK 1 hr 45 mins

Celery, saffron and white bean stew

Celery: always the bridesmaid, never the bride. Until, that is, the Persians came along and created *khoresh karafs*, a delicious celery stew. There is a whole head of it in this recipe, and an entire bunch of parsley, too. The celery is braised to velvet-soft submission, releasing immense flavor – somewhere between celery, shallots and fennel – that no one, not I, thought celery capable of. Traditionally, this stew is made with meat, but many Persians now make it using cannellini beans or potatoes.

NOTE If saffron is too much of a stretch for your budget, go without, but this is otherwise a very economical dish. Traditionally this is served with *tahdig* (Persian-style rice), but alternatives are steamed basmati mixed with a little vegan butter, salt and turmeric, if you like it yellow, or some crusty bread.

SERVES 4

20 strands of saffron

6 tbsp olive oil

1 yellow onion, *finely chopped*

1 x 1¼-lb bunch of celery, *stems cut at an angle into 1-inch pieces*

3 cloves of garlic, *crushed*

1 tsp ground turmeric

1¼ tsp salt

⅛ tsp ground black pepper

2 tbsp tomato paste

3½ oz fresh flat-leaf parsley, *trimmed, the rest finely chopped*

1 x 15-oz can of cannellini or navy beans, *not drained*

¾ oz fresh mint leaves, *finely chopped*

1 tbsp lemon juice, *from ½ lemon*

cooked basmati rice (p 305) **or fresh crusty bread,** *to serve*

Put the saffron into a little heatproof bowl, cover with 2 tablespoons of freshly boiled water and leave to one side.

Put the olive oil into a wide, deep frying pan over a medium heat and, when hot, add the onion and fry, stirring often, for 5 minutes. Add the celery, cook for 5 minutes more, then stir in the garlic, turmeric, salt and pepper, and cook for another 12 minutes.

Add the tomato paste, cook for a couple of minutes, then add the parsley and beans with their water (keep the can handy). Cook for 10 minutes, then add the mint and cook for a further 5 minutes.

Fill up the empty bean can with water from the tap, add this to the pan, then fill the can again, but only halfway this time, and add to the pan along with the lemon juice, saffron and its soaking water.

Simmer for 20 minutes, until the celery has gone from crunchy to tender, then almost soft, and the consistency is like a thickish stew. Take off the heat, taste and adjust the lemon juice and salt, if need be, then serve with rice or bread.

Carrot falafel with pickled onions

My love for falafel knows no bounds, but my love for deep-frying does. So this recipe is my offering for a baked falafel, as crunchy and crisp on the outside as the genuine article, and as soft and fluffy within. The key to all good falafel, I've learned, is to use dried chickpeas (canned ones turn to mush), which means you'll need to throw the chickpeas into a pot of water the day before. I usually soak them just before bedtime, so they can be turned into dinner the next day.

NOTE You'll need to soak the chickpeas a day before making. You'll also need a food processor for this recipe.

MAKES 20 falafel, to serve 4

falafel
1½ cups dried chickpeas
olive oil
7 oz peeled carrots, (from
  2 medium), *roughly chopped*
2 tbsp gram (chickpea) flour
3 cloves of garlic, *crushed*
1 tsp cumin seeds
1½ tsp coriander seeds
1½ tsp salt
½ tsp baking soda
2 tsp chilli flakes
2 tbsp chopped fresh
  flat-leaf parsley

pickled onions
1 red onion, *halved and finely sliced*
¼ cup white wine vinegar
1½ tsp salt

to serve
wraps or pita breads
hummus or vegan garlic "mayo"
thinly sliced English cucumber
sriracha sauce

Soak the chickpeas in a pan of cold water for 24 hours.

The next day, make the pickled onions first. Put the onion, vinegar and salt into a small saucepan, add ¼ cup of water and bring to a boil. Turn off the heat and leave to cool.

Preheat the oven to 425°F. Line two baking sheets with parchment paper and drizzle with olive oil.

Drain the chickpeas really thoroughly, then put them into a food processor with the carrots, gram flour, garlic, cumin seeds, coriander seeds, salt, baking soda, chilli flakes and parsley. Pulse until the mixture resembles a grainy paste, then take a spoonful of the mixture and roll it between your palms to check that it sticks together well. If it doesn't, pulse the mixture until it's finer, then test again. If the mixture feels too wet, add another tablespoon of gram flour. When you're happy, transfer to a bowl.

Take a ping pong ball–sized amount of the falafel mixture (roughly 1½ oz) and pack it as tight as you can between your hands, then gently flatten to around 2½ inches across x ¾ inch deep, patting the edges with a finger to neaten them up. Pop it onto the prepared baking sheet and repeat with the rest of the mixture.

Drizzle olive oil over the patties, then bake for 20 to 25 minutes, until crisp and golden.

Heat up some wraps or pita, spread lavishly with hummus or garlic "mayo," line with cucumber and the drained pickled onions, fill with falafel and finish with sriracha sauce, if you wish.

Thai yellow curry with green beans and potatoes

The traffic-light naming of Thai curries is perhaps a genius bit of marketing that has made their journey to Westerners' plates that much easier. While the green and red are defined by their corresponding chillies, the yellow is not, but instead is characterized by a stellar line-up of aromatics that includes lemongrass, turmeric, ginger, makrut lime leaves, cumin and coriander, which all come together like a beam of sunshine.

NOTE Buy the makrut lime leaves fresh or frozen from your local Chinese supermarket and store in the freezer. Waxy potatoes, like red potatoes and fingerlings, are better than starchy, as they soak up less sauce, but use whatever you have and add a little water to make it saucier if need be. You'll need a blender to make this.

SERVES 4

2 large shallots (2½ oz net), *roughly chopped*

1 whole head of garlic, *cloves separated and peeled*

2 stalks of lemongrass, *outer leaves and top third discarded, the rest roughly chopped*

1½ x 1½ inches ginger, *chopped*

4 bird's-eye chillies, *chopped*

4 makrut lime leaves

1 tsp ground turmeric

½ tsp ground cumin

1 tsp ground coriander

1½ tsp salt

2 x 14-oz cans of coconut milk

1¼ lbs waxy potatoes, *cut into 1½- x ¾-inch pieces*

2 tbsp canola oil

14 oz green beans, *topped*

cooked jasmine rice *(p 304), to serve*

First make the curry paste. Put the shallots, garlic, lemongrass, ginger, chillies, lime leaves, spices and salt into a blender, add ¼ cup of coconut milk, and blitz, adding an extra splash of coconut milk if you need, until you have a nice, smooth paste. Put to one side.

Bring a medium-sized saucepan of water to a boil, carefully lower in the potatoes and cook for 10 to 12 minutes, until a knife slips easily in and out. Drain and set aside while you start on the curry.

Put the oil into a large saucepan for which you have a lid, set it over a medium heat and, once hot, add the curry paste and stir-fry for 5 minutes; it will start to darken slightly and turn noticeably fragrant.

When the paste starts to look a little oily as the fat splits out of it, add the rest of the coconut milk and half a can of water. Bring to a simmer. Add the cooked potatoes and the green beans, bring everything back up to a simmer, cover and cook for 5 to 6 minutes longer, until the beans are tender and the curry has reduced and thickened slightly.

To serve, ladle the curry into bowls and serve with steamed jasmine rice.

V / GF   PREP 15 mins / COOK 30 mins

Roots, shoots and tubers

Parsnip and potato gnocchi with gochujang and hazelnuts

Consider the parsnip: fed to the pigs by the French and written out of Italian cuisine altogether. Unloved and overlooked, this root barely registers in British cooking, either, other than in the Christmas roast. But its sweet, starchy flesh can mash, crisp and roast as well as any potato. And here it binds a spell around flour to make excellent gnocchi, which work a charm with a hot-and-sour gochujang sauce.

NOTE Double to serve four. Gochujang is a sweet, hot Korean red pepper paste that can be found in most major supermarkets. Sweet white miso is sweeter than standard white miso.

SERVES 2

8½ oz peeled floury potato (from 1 large), *chopped*
5 oz peeled parsnip (from 2 medium), *chopped*
½ tsp salt
½ cup type 00 flour
1 tbsp gochujang paste
3 tbsp shiro or sweet white miso
2½ tbsp toasted sesame oil
2 tbsp lemon juice, *from 1 lemon*
1 tbsp canola oil
3½ oz baby spinach
⅓ cup toasted hazelnuts, *chopped*

Put the potato and parsnips into a medium-sized saucepan, cover with cold water and bring to a boil. Turn down to a simmer and cook for around 10 minutes, until tender or a knife slips through them easily. Drain in a colander and leave to steam dry, then tip back into the pan, add the salt and mash until very smooth.

Add the flour to the mash and, using your hands, gently mix it in to form a dough. Tip out onto a clean work surface and divide in two (keep the saucepan to one side). Roll each piece into a sausage around 14 inches long x ¾ inch thick, then cut each sausage into twelve even pieces.

Line a plate with a clean cloth and have a slotted spoon ready. Rinse out the saucepan and fill with fresh water. Bring to a rolling boil, drop in the gnocchi and cook for 1 to 2 minutes, until they float to the top. Lift out with the slotted spoon and drain on the lined plate.

In a small bowl, mix the gochujang, miso, sesame oil and lemon juice.

In a medium-sized frying pan, heat the canola oil, swirling the pan gently so it coats the base. Once hot, add the gnocchi and fry for a couple of minutes, until golden brown underneath. Flip over the gnocchi and cook for another couple of minutes, to brown the other side.

Add the spinach to the pan and stir gently (so as not to break up the gnocchi) until it wilts. Add the sauce, stir until the gnocchi and spinach are coated, then divide between two plates and scatter over the hazelnuts.

Pakistani-style aloo palak

When I took a break from my *Guardian* column to do what the Italians call "*dolce far niente*" (the sweet art of doing nothing), I was able to eat and cook selfishly, following my own desires. They took me to a Pakistani cafe where I found a potato and spinach curry I could eat every day for the rest of my life. The potatoes were salty and fudgy, like in a Spanish tortilla, and the spinach was an oily emerald tangle, having given up all hope of freshness. It wasn't innovative or pretty, but it hit the spot so perfectly, I nearly shouted, "Bingo!"

NOTE Frozen spinach works brilliantly here; either defrost overnight or run warm water over it, while still in the bag, until thawed.

SERVES 4

½ cup canola oil
1 tsp black mustard seeds
1 tsp cumin seeds
2 yellow onions, *finely chopped*
6 cloves of garlic, *crushed*
1 x ¾ inch ginger, *grated*
1–2 green finger (or serrano)
   chillies, *finely chopped*
7 oz tomatoes, *chopped*
1½ tsp ground cumin
2 tsp ground coriander
½ tsp ground turmeric
1 tsp Kashmiri chilli powder
2 tsp salt
1 lb Yukon Gold potatoes
   (2 medium), *peeled, halved and
   cut into ½-inch-thick slices*
2 lbs frozen whole leaf spinach,
   thawed
2–3 tsp lemon juice, *from 1 lemon*
cooked basmati rice *(p 305),
   to serve*

Put the oil into a large, deep pan over a medium heat until very hot, then carefully tip in the mustard and cumin seeds, and leave to fizz and crackle for up to a minute. Add the onions, cook for 8 minutes, until soft and golden, then add the garlic, ginger and chillies and cook, stirring, for about 3 minutes, until the raw garlic smell disappears.

Stir in the tomatoes, spices and salt, and cook for about 5 minutes, until you can see the oil separate from the tomato mixture. Add the potatoes, spinach and ¾ cup of just-boiled water, then pop the lid on the pan and leave to cook for about 15 minutes, stirring every 5 minutes or so. Take off the lid and cook for a final 15 minutes or until the liquid has been driven off and you are left with a lovely, thick curry with tender potatoes that don't resist a prodding from the tip of a knife.

Stir through 2 teaspoons of lemon juice, mix, then taste. Add some more lemon to balance the sweet and spicy flavors if need be, then serve hot with basmati rice.

Haggis keema with tattie rotis

Burns Night and my birthday are on the same day, and so it was just a matter of time before I merged Burns's love for haggis and tatties with my love of Indian keema and rotis, and so formed the inaugural Burns-Sodha birthday meal of haggis keema and tattie rotis. You could, if you wish, treat the haggis and roti recipes separately, and if you're short of time, you could always buy wheat rotis. The dish is built around a Macsween's vegan haggis, which you'll need to buy – it's widely available in most supermarkets in the UK. Depending on your location, you may be able to purchase one online.

SERVES 4

tattie rotis

1 lb peeled Yukon Gold potatoes
 (from 1¼ lbs unpeeled), *cut into
 1-inch cubes*
2 tbsp canola oil, *plus extra to fry
 the rotis*
salt
1 tsp nigella seeds
1⅔ cups all-purpose flour, *plus
 extra to dust*

haggis keema

3 tbsp canola oil
1 leek, *finely sliced*
1 large yellow onion, *finely
 chopped*
¾ x ¾ inch ginger, *grated*
5 cloves of garlic, *crushed*
2 green finger (or serrano) chillies,
 finely chopped
2 lbs vegan haggis
2 tsp ground coriander
2½ tsp ground cumin
½ tsp ground turmeric
½ cup plain Greek or dairy-free
 yogurt
½ oz fresh mint leaves, *chopped*
½ oz fresh cilantro leaves, *chopped*

Bring a medium-sized saucepan of water to a rolling boil, drop in the potatoes and cook for 12 minutes, or until tender. Drain and leave to dry in the colander. When dry, put the cooked potatoes back into the same pan, add the oil, a teaspoon of salt and the nigella seeds, and mash really well. Add the flour and knead with your hands until the mix comes together into a uniform ball of dough.

Lightly flour a work surface and put a large sheet of parchment paper to one side. Cut the roti dough into eight equal pieces. Take one piece of dough, roll it out into a 4-inch-diameter circle (sprinkling over extra flour if need be), then transfer to the paper and repeat with the remaining dough.

Put a plate next to the stove for the cooked rotis. Heat a teaspoon of oil in a wide nonstick frying pan over a medium heat, and, when hot, lay in as many rotis as you can comfortably fit (say, two) and cook for about 1½ minutes on each side, until blackened in places and there are no uncooked, doughy spots. Transfer to the plate. Repeat with the remaining rotis, cover with foil and set aside while you make the keema.

Put the oil for the keema into the same frying pan over a medium heat. When hot, add the leek and onion, and cook for about 8 minutes, until soft and translucent. Add the ginger, garlic and chillies, stir to mix, and cook for 2 minutes more.

Crumble in the haggis and cook, stirring frequently, for about 10 minutes— it may stick to the pan, but persevere. Stir in the ground coriander, cumin, turmeric and yogurt, cook for a further 5 minutes, then taste for seasoning. Add salt a ¼ teaspoon at a time, mixing and tasting after each addition, then stir in the fresh herbs. Serve hot with the rotis.

VO   PREP 20 mins / COOK 1 hr 15 mins

Chickpea and potato curry with quick paratha

Potato curry was the defining dish of my youth and, if I'm honest, I didn't love it back then (sorry, Mum). But, as sometimes happens with things you disliked as a child (antiques, Neil Diamond and my sister, for example), they come full circle and in later life you find an intense sort of love for them. Today's recipe isn't my family's potato curry, though; rather, it's one I made with an urge in my belly to feel at home again, and I was so pleased with the results that it might become a defining dish of my adult years.

NOTE You'll need makrut lime leaves for this and sambal oelek, a brilliantly zingy chilli paste. I buy both from my local Chinese supermarket. Pre-made frozen paratha can be found in Indian supermarkets, if you don't want to make your own. You'll need a blender or small food processor.

SERVES 4

curry
1 yellow onion, *roughly chopped*
2 tbsp tomato paste
5 cloves of garlic, *chopped*
2½ tbsp sambal oelek
8 fresh or frozen makrut lime leaves, *deveined*
canola oil
1½ tsp salt
2 x 15-oz cans of chickpeas, *not drained*
1 lb Yukon Gold potatoes, *peeled and cut into 1-inch pieces*
1 x 14-oz can of coconut milk

paratha
1 lb frozen puff pastry dough, *suitable for vegans, thawed*
all-purpose flour, *for dusting*

First make the curry paste. Put the onion, tomato paste, garlic, sambal oelek, 4 lime leaves and 5 tablespoons of oil into a blender or small food processor. Blitz to a smooth paste, stopping to scrape down the sides if need be. If your blender is struggling, add some water, a tablespoon at a time, to loosen the mixture. Leave to one side.

Roll up the remaining 4 lime leaves then cut them into shreds. Heat a tablespoon of oil in a large and deep frying pan and when the oil is very hot, briefly fry the lime leaves until crispy, then remove to a small plate. Scrape the paste into the pan and cook over a medium heat, stirring often, for about 10 to 12 minutes, until the paste starts to come away from the sides of the pan and it releases some of the oil back into the pan.

Stir in the salt, the chickpeas and their water, the potatoes and coconut milk, turn up the heat and bring to a boil, which should take about 5 minutes. Turn the heat to low and simmer for a further 20 minutes, stirring occasionally, until the potatoes are fudge-soft.

To make the paratha, clean and lightly flour a work surface. Divide the pastry dough into eight equal pieces. Roll each piece into a ball, then squash between your palms to form a patty. Coat both sides of the patty with flour, then roll out into an 7- to 8-inch round, and repeat with the remaining pastry.

Put a nonstick frying pan over a medium-high heat and, when hot, lay in the pastry round and cook for 1½ minutes, turning every 30 seconds, until dark brown spots appear and there is no visible uncooked (i.e., translucent) dough on either side. Transfer to a plate and repeat with the remaining dough.

Ladle the curry into a large bowl and scatter over the fried lime leaves. Serve with a big pile of parathas alongside and encourage people to help themselves.

V PREP 10 mins / COOK 55 mins

XL two-potato curry puffs

One potato, two potatoes, three potatoes, four, five potatoes, six potatoes*. . . curried, plus some coconut cream and puff pastry, and you have yourself some extra-large Malaysian curry puffs.

NOTE *You may not need six potatoes for this recipe but you will need a circular template for the puffs: an 8-inch-diameter plate or bottom of a cake pan will work perfectly.

SERVES 6

1¼ lbs potatoes, *peeled and cut into ½-inch cubes*

10 oz sweet potatoes, *peeled and cut into ½-inch cubes*

salt

3 tbsp canola oil

3 red onions, *diced*

4 cloves of garlic, *crushed*

2 x 1½ inches ginger (1½ oz), *grated*

3 red chillies, *finely chopped*

1½ tbsp mild curry powder

5 oz creamed coconut, *grated*

3 x 16-oz packages of ready-rolled puff pastry, vegan or all butter

1 medium egg, *whisked,* **or melted vegan butter,** *to glaze*

to serve
hot sauce, sriracha or ketchup
salad leaves

Put the potatoes and sweet potatoes into a medium-sized saucepan, cover with cold water, add a teaspoon of salt and bring to a boil. Cook for 10 minutes, drain and leave aside.

Next, heat the oil in a large sauté or frying pan over a medium heat, then add the onions and 1¼ teaspoons of salt. Sweat for 5 minutes, until translucent, then add the garlic, ginger and chillies. Cook for a further 5 minutes, until the onions are soft. Add the curry powder, mix well, then add the creamed coconut and mix again. Add the cooked potatoes, pour in 7 tablespoons of water and cook for 1 minute to bring all the flavors together; you should have a dry potato curry. Take off the heat and leave to cool while you cut out your pastry disks.

Preheat the oven to 425°F.

Work with one sheet at a time: Unroll the pastry sheet onto a clean surface, keeping the parchment paper underneath. Using your 8-inch template, cut out a disk. Repeat this process until you have 6 disks of equal size.

To fill the curry puffs, place 6 oz (or 2 large serving spoons) of the potato curry in the center of each disk of dough. Wet the edges of the dough with some water and bring the edge of dough nearest to you up and over the filling, stretching it if need be, before sealing it onto its opposite edge. Either pleat (by folding little sections of the dough up and over) or press shut with a fork. Place the puffs on a lined baking sheet and brush with the eggwash or some melted vegan butter.

Bake for 30 to 35 minutes, until lightly golden brown all over; they should give a nice rat-a-tat-tat sound when tapped. Allow to cool slightly before tucking in, and serve with your choice of red sauce and some salad leaves.

Rutabaga rasam

I'm very fond of rutabaga. It has a bit of the Cinderella narrative about it: often cast aside and underappreciated, but, when given attention and love, it blossoms. You can cook it in lots of different ways, but roasting it is my favorite approach. Then it becomes buttery and fondant-like, and in this recipe sits pretty in a gently sour, restorative split pea broth.

NOTE There are more split peas here than in a traditional rasam to make it more dinner friendly. Soak the split peas for 3 hours beforehand. If you forget, just increase the cooking time by up to 30 minutes and top up the water while cooking.

SERVES 4

1 cup split yellow peas
1 large rutabaga (2 lbs)
canola oil
salt
1 tsp black mustard seeds
¼ tsp fenugreek seeds
1 x 14-oz can of chopped
   tomatoes
2 tbsp tamarind paste
¼ tsp ground black pepper
1¼ tsp ground coriander
1¼ tsp ground cumin
1 tsp Kashmiri chilli powder
½ tsp ground turmeric
2 cloves of garlic, *finely sliced*
2 green finger (or serrano) chillies,
   halved lengthways

To serve
cooked basmati rice *(p 305)*

Put the split peas in a large bowl, wash well in a few changes of water, then drain. Cover with fresh cold water and leave to soak for 3 hours.

Preheat the oven to 425°F and line a large baking sheet with parchment paper.

Wash and peel the rutabaga, cut it into quarters, then cut each section into ½-inch-thick slices. Place in a bowl, pour over a tablespoon of oil and ¼ teaspoon of salt, and toss with your hands, so all the rutabaga is coated. Put on the baking sheet, bake for 30 minutes, or until the rutabaga is tender and browning, then remove and put to one side.

Put 2 tablespoons of oil into a large saucepan over a medium heat. When really hot, add the mustard and fenugreek seeds and cook for 30 seconds, until they pop. Add the drained split peas, pour in 5 cups of cold water, pop a lid on top, slightly cocked, then bring to a boil on a medium heat. Turn down the heat to low and leave to simmer, stirring occasionally, for 20 minutes, until the split peas are soft: they should have the consistency of cooked potato; if not, keep cooking until tender and top up the water if need be. Then stir in the tomatoes, tamarind paste, pepper, ground coriander, cumin, chilli powder, turmeric and 1¾ teaspoons of salt, and simmer for another 10 minutes, with the lid cocked.

Stir in two-thirds of the roasted rutabaga and cook for 6 minutes – don't worry if the rutabaga breaks up, it'll help thicken the rasam – then adjust the seasoning to taste, if need be.

Put 2 tablespoons of oil into a small pan over a medium heat and, when hot, add the garlic and chillies and fry for 2 minutes, or until the garlic is bronzed and the chillies are blistering white.

Pour the garlic and chilli mix into the rasam and mix, then decant into a deep dish or individual bowls. Top with the reserved rutabaga and serve with some steamed basmati rice.

Sweet squash and friends

Sweet squash and friends

Anshu's squash and corn erriseri

In Mumbai, up to 200,000 *dabbas*, containers of home-cooked food, are delivered from people's homes to workplaces every day by *dabbawalas*, who travel on foot or by bike. It's an epic story of India's love of home cooking. Thanks to Anshu Ahuja and her company, DabbaDrop, Londoners can eat her home cooking weekly, delivered by bike. This *erriseri* – a sweet, rich and sour stew – is a go-to recipe for Anshu's family: it's what her grandmother used to make for Sunday lunch, it's what her mother makes for guests and, now, it's what I make for my family and friends.

NOTE   You'll need a blender or immersion blender. Fresh curry leaves can be found in larger or Indian supermarkets and online (see p 310). Freeze what you don't use.

SERVES 4

1 butternut squash (2 lbs), *washed*
canola oil
salt
2 cups corn niblets (from a can), *drained*
2 tsp black mustard seeds
12 fresh curry leaves
1 large yellow onion, *finely chopped*
4 cloves of garlic, *crushed*
3 green finger (or serrano) chillies, *finely chopped*
2 tsp ground turmeric
1 x 14-oz can of coconut milk
2 tbsp lemon juice, *from 1 lemon*

to serve
a handful of fresh cilantro leaves
cooked basmati rice *(p 305)*
optional: lemon wedges and finely sliced red onion

Preheat the oven to 400°F.

Cut the squash in half (no need to peel), scoop out and discard the seeds, then cut it into ¾-inch cubes. Tip the squash pieces onto a baking sheet, pour over 2 tablespoons of oil and a good sprinkling of salt, and toss to coat. Bake for 25 to 30 minutes, until the squash chunks are tender and their edges caramelized.

Add 2 tablespoons of water to the drained corn kernels and blend to a smooth paste.

In a large frying pan, heat 2 tablespoons of oil and, when hot, add the mustard seeds and curry leaves, and leave them to crackle and pop for a minute. Now add the onion and cook, stirring occasionally, for about 10 minutes, until turning golden, then add the garlic and chillies, and cook for 2 minutes. Stir in the corn paste, turmeric and 1½ teaspoons of salt, cook for a minute, then add the coconut milk (keep the empty can handy) and whisk so everything is combined and the curry sauce is a vibrant yellow.

Half-fill the coconut milk can with water and add to the pot to loosen the curry – you may need a little more or less water than this, depending on the thickness of your coconut milk – then bring to a boil and simmer for 5 minutes, until it starts to thicken. Stir in the roast squash and lemon juice, and check the seasoning. Garnish with cilantro and serve with basmati rice, and lemon wedges and some sliced onion if you wish.

Tamarind tofu with noodles, herbs and pickles

Last summer, I returned from a sweltering trip to Bangkok straight into a steaming-hot British summer and instantly missed the incredible array of perfect hot-weather salads Thailand is famous for (and the air con), and needed to scratch the itch. The tamarind tofu is really a bonus – and it works very well – but you could easily make the noodles without it.

NOTE Mung bean glass noodles are very sympathetic in that they don't clump and break easily. Along with the pickled sushi ginger, they can be found in Chinese supermarkets. Not all vegan fish sauces are equal (Tofuna makes a good one). A julienne peeler will make light work of the zucchini.

SERVES 4

tofu

1¼ lbs extra-firm tofu, *drained*
3 tbsp tamarind paste
2 tbsp agave or brown rice syrup
½ tsp salt
canola oil

salad

3½ oz dried mung bean noodles
1 medium zucchini, *julienned*
5¼ oz bean sprouts
⅓ iceberg lettuce, *shredded*
¾ oz pickled sushi ginger
1 oz mixed fresh mint and
 Thai basil, *leaves picked*
6 tbsp store-bought crispy fried
 onions
5 tbsp salted peanuts, *crushed*

dressing

2 tbsp vegan fish sauce
2 tbsp agave or brown rice syrup
2–3 bird's-eye chillies, *finely
 chopped*
2 tbsp lime juice, *from 2 limes*
¼ tsp salt

Pat the tofu dry with paper towel, cut into ½-inch slices then into triangles. Put a fresh sheet of paper towel on a plate near the stove.

Make up a glaze in a small bowl by whisking the tamarind paste, syrup and salt with 2 tablespoons of water, then put to one side.

Heat a layer of oil in a nonstick frying pan and, when it's very hot, add half the tofu in a single layer. Fry for 6 to 7 minutes, turning once halfway, until golden brown on both sides, then transfer to the paper-lined plate, and repeat with the remaining tofu.

Turn down the heat and remove most of the oil from the pan – you don't want more than a tablespoon left in – then pour in the tamarind glaze and return all the tofu to the pan. Cook for about 3 minutes, until the glaze bubbles over the tofu, and turn the pieces so they're all coated. When there's little glaze left in the pan, take off the heat and leave to cool.

Make up the dressing by combining the vegan fish sauce, syrup, chillies, lime juice and salt. Cook the noodles according to the package instructions, rinse under cold water, then drain really well.

Only assemble just before serving. Put all the salad ingredients except the fried onions, peanuts and noodles in a bowl. Add the cooked noodles and dressing, and toss (the easiest way to do this is with your hands, pulling the ingredients up from the bottom of the bowl). Toss through the tofu and half each of the fried onions and peanuts, then distribute across four plates. Top with the remaining peanuts and fried onions, and serve.

Soy pickled pumpkin and chestnut maze gohan

Maze gohan, or mixed rice, is a mingling of sticky, sweet, short-grain rice studded with pickled ingredients seasoned with dashi and soy. It's both a delight for the senses and the perfect mix of comfort and joy.

NOTE There are many excellent edible pumpkins and squashes, but for flavor, my favorites are acorn, Crown Prince, Delica and Kabocha. If they're out of season, use butternut squash.

SERVES 2

1½ cups short-grain rice

¼ tsp salt

¼ cup light soy sauce

3 tbsp rice vinegar

1 tbsp cooking sake

2 tbsp toasted sesame oil

5 cloves of garlic, *halved lengthways*

5 scallions, *finely sliced*

5 oz fresh shiitake mushrooms, *sliced*

16 oz pumpkin or squash, *peeled and cut into ½-inch cubes*

3½ oz cooked chestnuts, *sliced*

Place the rice in a medium-sized saucepan for which you have a tight-fitting lid, and cover with warm water. Agitate the rice with your hand until the water turns cloudy, then drain and repeat, until the water runs clear. Cover with warm water, leave to soak for 5 minutes, then drain well.

Return the rice to the pan, cover with 1⅔ cups of cold water, add ¼ teaspoon of salt, cover with the lid and bring to a boil. Turn down to a simmer, cook for 10 minutes, then take off the heat and leave to rest, still covered, for 10 minutes more.

Meanwhile, make the pickling liquid. Mix the soy sauce, vinegar and sake in a little bowl and put to one side.

Put the sesame oil into a wide frying pan for which you have a lid and set it over a medium heat. When hot, add the garlic and cook, stirring, for 2 minutes. Next, add the scallions (reserve some of the greens for later), stir to mix and cook for 2 minutes more. Add the mushrooms, cook for 5 minutes, until sweated down, then add the pickling liquid, pumpkin and chestnuts. Cover the pan, leave to cook for 3 minutes, stir, then pop the lid back on and leave to cook for another 3 minutes, or until the pumpkin is tender.

Using a fork (so as not to mash the rice), scrape the rice into the vegetable pan and gently mix everything together. Either serve in the pan or distribute between bowls, with the reserved scallion greens scattered over.

Sweet squash and friends

Squash, cashew and tamarind curry

One of my favorite earthly pleasures is a Thai curry. For years, my first choice was green curry, but after a recent trip to Phuket, that has been trumped by *gaeng som*, or hot-and-sour curry. The original dish is clear and soupy, which works in the searing Thai sun, but I've added some cashews here to give it a silky and rich sauce that's better suited to the more inclement British weather.

NOTE Not all vegan fish sauces are equal (Tofuna makes a good one). You'll need a blender.

SERVES 4

⅔ cup roasted unsalted cashews
1 butternut squash (2 lbs)
canola oil
salt
7 large shallots (8½ oz net), *roughly chopped*
8 cloves of garlic, *chopped*
4 bird's-eye chillies, *chopped*
1½ x 1½ inches ginger, *chopped*
1½ tsp ground turmeric
3 limes: *2 juiced, to get 2 tbsp; the other cut into wedges*
1 tbsp superfine sugar
¼ cup tamarind paste
3 tbsp vegan fish sauce
7 oz rainbow chard, *stems cut into ¾-inch pieces, leaves cut into ribbons*
cooked jasmine rice *(p 304), to serve*

Preheat the oven to 425°F and line a baking sheet with parchment paper.

Put the cashews into a small heatproof bowl, cover with boiling water and set aside to soak.

Top and tail the squash, then cut first across the belly and then into quarters. Scoop out and discard (or repurpose) the seeds, then cut each quarter into 1½-inch-wide wedges. Rub 2 tablespoons of oil over the wedges, sprinkle with salt and lay them on the lined baking sheet. Bake for 15 minutes, flip onto the other side, bake for another 15 minutes, then remove from the oven.

Now for the curry paste. Drain the cashews and put them into a blender with the shallots, garlic, chillies, ginger, turmeric, lime juice, sugar, 6 tablespoons of water, 3 tablespoons of oil and 1½ teaspoons of salt. Blitz to a paste.

Put ¼ cup of oil into a large pan over a medium heat and, once hot, scrape in the paste from the blender. Cook, stirring often, for 5 minutes, then add the tamarind paste, vegan fish sauce and 4 cups of water. Stir, then add the chard and the roast squash, and bring the mixture up to a bubble. Turn down the heat to a simmer for 8 minutes, or until the chard stalks are tender, then taste and adjust the seasoning, adding more fish sauce for saltiness or lime, if you wish.

To serve, spoon the rice into bowls and ladle the curry over the top. Cut the remaining lime into wedges and serve on the side.

Japanese keema curry with zucchini fritters

In culinary history, the military has played a surprising role in helping ideas (and recipes) to travel across the world. Curry, for example, arrived in Japan not via India, as you might expect, but via the British military in the late 1800s, and caught on to such an extent that it is a household staple in Japan today. It's very different from a typical Indian curry in that it uses curry powder, is not particularly spicy and is thickened with flour. Keema means "ground meat" in Hindi; here I've used textured soy protein (TSP).

N O T E The fritters are optional; fried eggs make a good substitute. If you can't find S&B curry powder, use 2 tablespoons of regular curry powder.

SERVES 4

keema curry
8 dried shiitake mushrooms (¾ oz)
4 oz textured soy protein (TSP)
2 tbsp canola oil
1 yellow onion, *finely chopped*
2 large carrots (7 oz), *finely diced*
2 stalks of celery, *finely diced*
1¼ tsp salt
1½ tbsp S&B or 2 tbsp regular
   curry powder
¼ cup all-purpose flour
2 tbsp tomato ketchup
1 tbsp dark soy sauce
1 tbsp rice vinegar

fritters
3 tbsp cornstarch
¼ cup all-purpose flour
½ cup sparkling water
1 small zucchini, *trimmed*
3½ oz scallions, *trimmed*
canola oil, *to cook*
flaky sea salt, *to finish*

cooked jasmine rice *(p 304),*
   to serve

Place the mushrooms in a heatproof pitcher and pour over 2 cups of freshly boiled water. Next, place the TSP in a heatproof bowl and cover with up to 4 cups of freshly boiled water. Leave both to soak for 5 minutes, then squeeze out the mushrooms, keeping the stock, and finely chop them. Drain and press the TSP in a sieve, discarding the soaking water, and leave to one side.

Put the oil for the curry into a frying pan over a medium to high heat and, when hot, add the onion, carrots, celery, chopped mushrooms and the salt. Cook for 15 minutes, or until soft, then add the curry powder and flour, stirring constantly for a minute to cook out the flour, then stir in the drained TSP. Little by little, add the shiitake stock, leaving behind the last tablespoon in case of grit. Let the mixture bubble, then stir through the ketchup, soy sauce and vinegar. Cook for another 2 minutes, then take off the heat and set aside.

To make the fritters, put the cornstarch and flour into a mixing bowl and whisk in the sparkling water. Peel the zucchini with a vegetable peeler into thin strips until you have 3½ oz, and finely slice the scallions into long, thin strips, then mix into the batter. Line a plate with paper towel and leave to one side of the stove.

Put ¼ cup of oil into a nonstick frying pan over a medium to high heat. When it's very hot (test with a wooden spoon: if bubbles form around the edge, it's ready), scoop up a quarter of the zucchini mixture with a (clean) hand, leaving the batter behind, and drop into the hot oil. Pick up another quarter and do the same. Gently flatten the fritters using a fish spatula and cook for 3 minutes, flipping every minute until golden brown. Remove to a plate, sprinkle with sea salt and repeat with the remaining batter, adding more oil if need be.

Reheat the curry if it's cooled, and divide the rice and curry between four bowls or plates, topping with the zucchini fritters.

V   PREP 15 mins / COOK 45 mins

Kiri hodi with butternut squash

Kiri hodi, or coconut milk curry, is one of Sri Lanka's most popular dishes – and it is a genius recipe. All you need to do to create this taste of paradise, made using a combination of spices, citrus and coconut milk, is to bung the ingredients into a pot and the squash into the oven. It's the perfect thing to cook for time-poor or weary cooks, and the perfect thing to eat to bring some big tropical energy into your life.

NOTE The roast butternut is untraditional, but it lends sweetness to the creamy sourness of kiri hodi and also adds substance. Fresh curry leaves can be found in larger supermarkets. Freeze any leftovers for next time.

SERVES 4

- 2 lbs butternut squash, *peeled, seeded, then cut into ½-inch cubes*
- 2 tsp mild curry powder
- 1½ tbsp canola oil
- salt
- 1 yellow onion, *finely diced*
- 5 green finger (or serrano) chillies, *finely sliced*
- 12–15 fresh curry leaves
- ¾ tsp ground turmeric
- ½ tsp fenugreek seeds
- 5 cloves of garlic, *crushed*
- 5 oz cherry tomatoes, *halved*
- 1 long cinnamon stick, *snapped in two*
- 2 x 14-oz cans of coconut milk
- 1½ tbsp lime juice, *from 1 lime, or to taste*

- cooked basmati rice *(p 305), to serve*

Preheat the oven to 400°F and line a baking sheet with parchment paper.

Put the squash cubes into a large bowl, add the curry powder, oil and ¾ teaspoon of salt, and toss to coat. Tip out onto the baking sheet in an even layer, roast for 35 minutes, then take out of the oven and set aside to cool.

Meanwhile, put the onion, chillies, curry leaves, turmeric, fenugreek seeds, garlic, cherry tomatoes, cinnamon and 1½ teaspoons of salt into a medium-sized saucepan, then add ¾ cup of water. Over a medium to high heat, bring up to a boil and cook for 10 to 12 minutes, until the onions and tomatoes are completely soft and nearly all the liquid has evaporated.

Add the coconut milk and the roast squash, bring back to a bubbling simmer, then turn off the heat and add the lime juice. Taste and adjust the salt and lime as needed, and mash the squash if you'd like to thicken the curry. Serve hot over freshly steamed rice.

Whole squash biryani

This is a perfect dish for sharing at Christmas time, but especially on Christmas Day. It can be served as a main course, but the spices and flavors are sympathetic enough to go alongside a traditional roast. The type of squash you buy is key here. Delica is the best for flavor and sweetness, but a large kabocha squash or even crown pumpkin would also work (avoid the big orange pumpkins, though – they're great for carving scary faces into but not very nice for eating).

NOTE Pre-mixed basmati and wild rice can be bought in most major supermarkets. You'll need a pestle and mortar or something heavy to bash the spices with.

SERVES 4–6

¾ cup basmati and wild rice
3 to 3½ lb whole delica squash
salt
1 tsp fennel seeds
1 tsp cumin seeds
¾ tsp ground cinnamon
canola oil
1 large yellow onion, *finely sliced*
4 cloves of garlic, *crushed*
¾ x ¾ inch ginger, *grated*
1 tbsp tomato paste
1½ tsp Kashmiri chilli powder
1 cup vegetable stock, *plus*
    5 tsp water
⅓ cup walnuts (i.e., a big handful),
    chopped
3½ oz cranberry sauce

Preheat the oven to 350°F. Place the rice in a bowl, cover with cold water, then swirl it around with your hand, drain and repeat, until the water runs clear. Drain again, then cover with cold water and leave to soak.

Cut the top off the squash – keep the lid – and scoop out and discard the seeds (or keep to roast); if you've scooped out any flesh, dice and put it to one side. Crush the fennel and cumin seeds in a mortar until fairly well ground, then add the cinnamon. Keep to one side.

Heat 3 tablespoons of oil in a frying pan on a medium heat, then add the bashed spices and onion, and cook, stirring, for 12 minutes, until dark brown. Set aside a tablespoon of the onion mix, stir the garlic and ginger into the pan, then add the diced squash flesh, if any, the tomato paste and a teaspoon of chilli powder. Cook for 3 to 4 minutes, until the mixture is dry, then add ¾ teaspoon of salt, the well-drained rice and the vegetable stock and water. Bring to a boil and cook for 6 minutes, then take off the heat, mix in the walnuts and spoon the lot into the squash.

Put the reserved onion mixture on top of the rice and close with the squash lid. Wrap the squash tightly in foil like a badly wrapped present, put on a baking sheet and bake for 1 hour and 10 minutes, or until a knife slips through the side very easily and the rice is cooked.

Mix the cranberry sauce with a tablespoon of oil and the remaining ½ teaspoon of chilli powder. Unwrap the squash, put on a fancy platter, cut into wedges and serve with the cranberry "chutney."

V / GF   PREP 10 mins / COOK 1 hr 55 mins

Dinner essentials
Condiments

*The sauce is the boss!**

There are very few things mankind cannot live without. But for me, life would be unimaginable without pickles, sauces and chutneys. Here are five of my must-haves:

1. Chilli crisp

Chilli crisp already has a cult following, but it is still the best gift to mealtimes available in a jar. Describing it as a chilli condiment would be like describing Elton John as a pop singer; it's technically correct but doesn't capture how all-encompassing it is – just one spoonful hits all the mouth's pleasure buttons: salty, sweet, spicy (but not hot), crunchy, chewy and savory.

I use it in multiple ways: to make a sauce, to stir into noodles, and to top congee, dumplings or silken tofu. I like to pimp mayonnaise with it, have it over eggs and mix it into cooked greens. There are several brands of chilli condiments now, but Lao Gan Ma's original chilli crisp remains my favorite. The runner-up is its "kohlrabi, peanuts and tofu in chilli oil," which is richer and more textured, like a Ben and Jerry's ice cream, and tastes tomato-ier. In third place, its "preserved black beans in chilli oil." They're not interchangeable, they vary in heat and saltiness, so always add a little at a time until it tastes right.

You can find it in your Chinese supermarket or online (pro tip: go for the 24-ounce jar, you won't regret it). Use it to make: roasted eggplant with silken tofu (p 33), Xi'an-style pappardelle (p 91) and sesame noodles with spicy fried "meat" (p 231).

*The motto of my favorite BBQ sauce, Sweet Baby Ray's.

2. Mayonnaise

In the kingdom of mayonnaise, Kewpie is king. Created by Toichiro Nakashima in 1924, it's now a household staple in Japan. He was looking to create a more nutritious version of the one he encountered in America, and though I wouldn't say that it's good for you, it's made using only the yolk (rather than the whole egg), giving it a richer mouthfeel and greater intensity than your average mayonnaise, while the blend of vinegars, apple and wine makes it sweeter. Overall the effect is like trading up from the boy next door to the more handsome, more charming hunk down the road.

I enjoy using the slim nozzle of my Kewpie bottle to criss-cross over my okonomiyaki, sushi, sandwiches, tofu and greens. Everything, really.

3. Sambal oelek chilli paste

Sambal oelek is to hot sauce what sparkling wine is to champagne. Hailing from Indonesia but also used widely in Malaysia and Singapore, it's sweeter, chirpier, brighter and palatable even by self-proclaimed chilli haters. You can eat it as it is over greens, noodles or eggs, or use it in the base of a curry or soup (like in my chickpea and potato curry on p 190) to create some depth and heat. In short, you can use it like a lazy person's fresh chilli or whenever your dish is missing a certain something – most likely that something will be sambal oelek. If you can't find sambal oelek in stores, it's easy to make yourself or you can substitute an equal amount of chilli garlic sauce.

4. Kimchi

"Cabbage surprise" is what kimchi could otherwise be called, the surprise being that it's so addictive and probably responsible for the Koreans eating 104 pounds of cabbage per person per year.** A napa style of leafy cabbage is the main ingredient (although other types of vegetable kimchi exist), followed swiftly by sea salt, ginger, garlic and gochugaru (Korean red pepper flakes). The mixture is fermented for a few days and the result is tang and spice in equal measure: two great qualities to help your taste buds and meals reach their full flavor potential. Mother-in-Law's makes a wonderful kimchi.

**statista.com

Use straight out of the jar in a cheese sandwich or dan bing (p 112) or make a sauce for your spaghetti, frying the kimchi first to mellow out the flavors (p 218). Make sure to check the label if you're vegetarian, as some brands contain fish sauce.

5. Mango chutney

I love Geeta's mango chutney, and considering how much real estate it occupies in my mind and fridge, I'm surprised it's only been around since the 1990s. For raw mango pickle, no one trumps my grandma, but Geeta plays the ace with her chutney. The reason it's so good is twofold: in many ways it tastes like the perfect mango – 60% sweet and 40% sour – but it also has a lovely authentic feel about it that makes me feel like it could have been made by an aunty: the whole peppercorns, chunks of garlic and onion seeds strike pitch-perfect notes. Use with any sort of cheese at any sort of time — see p 101 for my sticky mango and lime paneer naans, for example.

Pantrying

Kimchi and tomato spaghetti

Kimchi has a split personality. When I eat it raw, its crunchy sourness creeps toward my eyes, slapping them shut with a wince. It's addictive, like sour sweets. But cooked to just shy of caramelized, as in this recipe, the cabbage softens, its inner sweetness is released and the rowdy sourness mellows to a point where it only causes me to raise an eyebrow.

NOTE Gochugaru is Korea's main squeeze when it comes to chilli. It smells sweet, like dehydrated strawberries, and has a medium heat. Find it at your local East Asian supermarket or online (p 310). Buy the best kimchi you can find.

SERVES 4

kimchi spaghetti
2 tbsp canola oil
2 tbsp toasted sesame oil, *plus extra to serve*
3 cloves of garlic, *crushed*
5 oz kimchi, *drained and finely chopped*
2 tsp gochugaru flakes
2 tsp agave or brown rice syrup
1 x 14-oz can of chopped tomatoes
salt
14 oz spaghetti

breadcrumbs
½ cup unseasoned dried breadcrumbs
2 tbsp pine nuts
1½ tbsp raw black sesame seeds

Pour the canola oil and a tablespoon of toasted sesame oil into a medium-sized saucepan over a medium heat and, when hot, add the garlic and cook for 2 minutes, until pale gold. Add the kimchi and stir-fry for a few minutes, until all the water has been driven off and the oil has visibly separated.

Stir in the gochugaru and syrup, then add the tomatoes and bring to a bubble. Turn down the heat, cock a lid over the top (as the sauce thickens, it may spit), and leave to cook for 15 to 20 minutes, stirring occasionally, until it has thickened nicely. Season to taste (the saltiness of kimchi will vary – I use ¾ to 1 teaspoon of salt).

In the meantime, make the breadcrumbs. Put the remaining tablespoon of sesame oil into a small frying pan over a low to medium heat and, when hot, add the breadcrumbs, pine nuts and sesame seeds, and stir-fry until the breadcrumbs are crisp and golden. Stir through a pinch or two of salt and transfer to a bowl.

Fill a very large pan with water, season with salt (I use a teaspoon of salt for every 4 cups of water) and bring to a boil. Cook the spaghetti according to the package instructions and, just before draining, scoop out a small mug of the cooking water and put to one side.

Tip the drained pasta into the sauce and toss using a spaghetti spoon or tongs, adding a few tablespoons of pasta water if the sauce needs loosening. Check for seasoning and adjust as you see fit.

Fork the spaghetti out onto a serving plate (or onto four separate plates), sprinkle the sesame breadcrumbs liberally over the top and drizzle over a little more sesame oil, if you wish.

V   PREP 5 mins / COOK 30 mins

Koshari

Koshari is as popular across Egypt as its pyramids are across the world. Although no one knows exactly where the dish originated, one theory is that it was inspired by kitchari, the spiced Indian rice and lentil dish. But as well as rice and lentils, koshari contains pasta and is topped with a sharp tomato sauce and fried onions. Whatever its origin, what's certain is that it can be cooked using mostly pantry ingredients and will be as popular on your kitchen table as it is on the streets of Cairo.

SERVES 4

1 cup basmati rice
canola oil
2 red onions, *halved and thinly sliced*
salt
4 cloves of garlic, *crushed*
1 x 14-oz can of chopped tomatoes
1½ tsp chilli flakes
2 tsp white wine vinegar
6 oz dried brown lentils
5 oz macaroni
1 tsp ground cumin
1 tsp ground cinnamon
1¼ cups vegetable stock

Wash the rice thoroughly under the cold tap until the water runs clear, then leave to soak in plenty of cold water.

Heat 6 tablespoons of oil in a frying pan over a medium heat and, when hot, add the onions and 2 pinches of salt. Fry, stirring regularly, for 30 minutes, until dark brown and sticky. Scoop out the onions with a slotted spoon, pressing them against the side of the pan to drain them of as much oil as possible, and transfer to a plate lined with paper towel.

Reheat the oil in the pan (there should be about ¼ cup left) on a medium heat, then fry the garlic for 3 minutes, until it starts to turn golden. Stir in the tomatoes and their juices, ⅔ cup of water and ½ teaspoon of salt, and cook for 20 minutes, stirring infrequently. Add the chilli flakes and vinegar, then turn off the heat.

Meanwhile, put the lentils into a large saucepan for which you have a tight-fitting lid. Cover with plenty of cold water, bring to a boil and simmer for 15 minutes. Then add the macaroni, and cook for a minute less than your package says. Drain well, then tip into a large mixing bowl and cover loosely with foil to keep warm.

Drain the soaked rice. In the same pan you used to cook the lentils, heat 2 tablespoons of oil on a medium heat, then add the rice, cumin, cinnamon and 1½ teaspoons of salt, and stir to coat the rice, being careful not to burn the spices. After a couple of minutes, slowly add the stock, bring it to a boil, pop the lid on, turn down to a simmer and leave to cook undisturbed for 10 minutes. Turn off the heat and leave, still covered, to rest for 10 minutes.

Add most of the onions (leaving a handful aside) to the lentils and macaroni and gently mix in the rice, then transfer to a serving platter. Top with the tomato sauce and the remaining onions, and serve.

Bun cha with "meatballs"

This is the kind of dish that makes a Tuesday night feel like a Friday, a summer's night feel like an endless year, and a long hard week feel like a minute. On paper, it might not look like a simple recipe, but most of the ingredients are dispatched into a bowl, pan or plate quickly and easily.

NOTE You'll need a quality vegan fish sauce (Tofuna makes a good one), and a stir-fry sauce called "mushroom vegetarian stir-fry sauce" made by Lee Kum Kee. Both can be found in major (or Chinese) supermarkets. You may need a food processor to bring the "meatballs" together if they don't come together naturally.

SERVES 4

dressing
2 tbsp lime juice, *from 2 limes*
2 cloves of garlic, *crushed*
1 bird's-eye chilli, *finely chopped*
3 tbsp vegan fish sauce
1½ tbsp soft light brown sugar

salad
3½ oz rice vermicelli noodles
2 carrots (5 oz), *peeled*
¼ daikon radish or ½ zucchini (5 oz)
½ iceberg lettuce (5 oz), *shredded*
1½ oz fresh mint, *leaves picked*
¼ cup store-bought crispy fried
    onions

"meatballs"
3½ oz textured soy protein (TSP)
1 tbsp vegan fish sauce
1 stalk of lemongrass, *outer leaves
    and top third discarded, the rest
    finely chopped*
2 tbsp mushroom vegetarian
    stir-fry sauce
2½ tbsp cornstarch
¼ cup unseasoned dried
    breadcrumbs
2 scallions, *very finely sliced*
2 cloves of garlic, *crushed*
canola oil, *for frying*

First, combine all the dressing ingredients in a small bowl and mix together with 2 tablespoons of water.

To make the salad, cook the noodles according to the package instructions. Drain and rinse in a sieve under the cold tap to stop them cooking, then leave to one side. Using a julienne peeler, peel the carrot and radish or zucchini into long strips, or cut into long matchsticks. Place them in a bowl, add the lettuce and half the mint, and mix.

To make the "meatballs," place the TSP in a large heatproof bowl and pour over ⅔ cup of freshly boiled water. Leave for 2 minutes, stir, then add the other "meatball" ingredients, apart from the oil. Mix really well, and check that the mixture can be formed into a ball easily. If it can't, tip it into a food processor and pulse until it comes together nicely. Separate the mixture into four equal mounds, then divide each mound into quarters, so you have sixteen piles. Take your first quarter, compress, roll into a ball, press down with your palms to form a pattie around ½ inch thick, and place to one side. Repeat with the rest of the mixture.

Heat 3 tablespoons of oil in a frying pan and, when hot, cook the patties in batches for 8 minutes each, turning every couple of minutes to make sure they don't get too dark on the outside.

To assemble the salad, place half the noodles on a platter, followed by half the vegetables, half the crispy fried onions, then the remaining noodles and vegetables. Top with the patties, then scatter over the remaining mint leaves and crispy fried onions. Finally, spoon over the dressing.

Fried tofu over tomato sambal with coconut rice

Classic. Spot-hitting. Dinner material.

SERVES 4

5 oz English cucumber (around ½ a large)
3 tbsp rice vinegar
salt
canola oil
3½ tbsp ancho chilli flakes
6 cloves of garlic, *crushed*
2 x 14-oz cans of chopped tomatoes
1 tbsp superfine sugar
1⅛ cups jasmine rice
1 x 14-oz can of coconut milk
1¼ lbs extra-firm tofu, *drained*
5 tbsp cornstarch
½ tsp Chinese five-spice powder
⅓ cup salted peanuts, *ground in a pestle and mortar or finely chopped*

First, make the cucumber pickle. Cut the cucumber in half lengthways, scoop out the seeds using a teaspoon and discard, then slice into thin— say ⅛ inch – half-moons. Put the cucumber into a bowl with the vinegar and ½ teaspoon of salt, mix to combine and leave to one side.

Next, get the sambal going. Put 6 tablespoons of oil, the ancho chilli flakes and the garlic into a saucepan, stir and set over a medium heat. When the garlic turns a pale gold and the chilli flakes crisp and sizzle (which may take around a minute), add the tomatoes, sugar and 1½ teaspoons of salt. Mix, cover with a three-quarter cocked lid and leave to bubble away over a gentle heat, stirring every now and then, for around 12 minutes, until rich, thick and delicious.

In the meantime, put the rice into a sieve and wash it thoroughly under the cold tap until the water runs clear. Put into a pan with the coconut milk, ⅔ cup of water and ½ teaspoon of salt, bring up to a boil, then cover the pan and turn down the heat to a whisper. Leave to cook for 15 minutes, then turn off the heat and leave, lid on, to steam.

Pat the tofu blocks dry with paper towel, then cut them in half lengthways to form four slabs (roughly 2½ x 2½ x 1 inch).

Mix the cornstarch, five-spice powder and ½ teaspoon of salt on a flat dish with a lip. Coat each side of the tofu slabs with the mixture, then transfer to a second plate. Put a thin layer of oil into a nonstick pan over a medium to high heat, lower in as many tofu blocks as will comfortably fit, and fry for 4 minutes on each side, or until golden and crisp, frying the edges by holding the tofu with tongs. Repeat with the remaining tofu.

To serve each portion, scoop a quarter of the rice into a small bowl, pack well and place a dinner plate over the top, then carefully flip upside down. Place a generous spoonful of sambal on the rice, then put a tofu block on top and add another spoonful of sambal. Decorate with the cucumber pickle and crushed peanuts.

Tiger roll sushi

My old boss used to say that England was such a productive country on account of its cold winters. And he had a point, because the colder months are when I tackle more interesting things in the kitchen, like marmalade, bread-baking and sushi, all of which create a sense of reward to counter the dark and short days. And just because sushi is more of a "project" doesn't mean it's difficult. For this dish, the only thing you need to cook is the rice; the rest – vegetables, tofu, avocado – is a chopping, mixing and assembly job. So, as recipes go, there's a decent margin for error.

NOTE The name "tiger" comes from the stripes painted on top of the roll. It is not authentic, but it is fun. You can buy sriracha mayonnaise widely (it's vegan), but if you can't find it, mix a tablespoon of sriracha with 2 tablespoons of vegan mayonnaise.

SERVES 4

1½ cups sushi or short-grain rice
3 tbsp rice vinegar
4 tsp superfine sugar
1½ tsp salt
¼ small red cabbage, *shredded*
1 large carrot, *peeled and cut into matchsticks*
4 sheets of nori
4 oz smoked tofu, *cut into ½-inch-thick batons*
1 avocado, *peeled and cut into ½-inch-thick batons*
3 tbsp sriracha mayonnaise
¼ cup store-bought crispy fried onions

Put the rice into a small pan, cover with lukewarm water, then agitate with your hand until the water turns cloudy. Drain and repeat until the water runs clear. Cover with warm water, leave to soak for 5 minutes, then drain again.

Return the rice to the pan and cover with 1⅔ cups of cold water. Put on the lid, bring to a boil, then turn down the heat to a whisper and cook for 10 minutes. Turn off the heat and leave to steam, lid still on, for 10 minutes more.

In a small bowl, mix 2 tablespoons of the vinegar with the sugar and a teaspoon of salt to make the sushi seasoning. Stir this through the cooked rice, then cover again to keep it warm.

In a bowl, toss the cabbage and carrot with the last tablespoon of vinegar and ½ teaspoon of salt and set aside.

Lay a sheet of parchment paper on a worktop. Put a sheet of nori down on the paper and spread a quarter of the rice all over the top, leaving a ¾-inch gap at the top end – this will make the sushi easier to roll. Put a horizontal line of cabbage and carrot in the center, on top of the rice at the end nearest to you, then lay a line of tofu and avocado in the middle of the rice. Wet the open end of the nori with a little water and, using the paper for support, roll as tightly as possible away from you to create a sealed roll. Repeat with the remaining nori and filling.

With your sharpest knife, cut each roll into eight, then push them back together again to recreate a single roll. Put on a platter, drizzle over the sriracha mayo, top with crispy fried onions and serve.

Vodka gochujang pasta

Sometimes I find myself projecting into dinner what I really want out of life – and this pasta has some really big energy about it. It's so extra, it's the type of thing you should be eating in your bikini while drinking a magnum of rosé, not in Hebden Bridge (or wherever you live), but on a beach on Mykonos. In short, I want a little bit more of what this pasta has to offer.

NOTE Gochujang is a sweet, hot, Korean red pepper paste that is sold in most major supermarkets. It's not blow-your-socks-off hot, especially when tempered with cream.

SERVES 4

2 tbsp canola oil
1 red onion, *halved and thinly sliced*
1 tsp salt
2 cloves of garlic, *crushed*
1¾ cups passata or finely chopped canned tomatoes
1 tbsp gochujang paste
1 tbsp tomato paste
6 tbsp vodka
¾ cup table (18%) cream or oat-based creamer
14 oz rigatoni
black pepper, *to serve*

Put the oil into a large frying pan on a medium to high heat, add the onion and salt, and cook, stirring, for 8 minutes, until the onion is soft enough to cut easily with a wooden spoon.

Add the garlic, fry for 2 minutes, then add the passata, gochujang, tomato paste and half the vodka, and leave it all to bubble away for 10 minutes, until the mix is quite paste-like. Stir in the cream and the rest of the vodka, simmer for a couple of minutes, then take off the heat.

Cook the rigatoni for a minute less than the package instructions. Carefully scoop a mug (around 1 cup) of the cooking water out of the pasta pan, put this to one side, then drain the pasta.

Pop the sauce back on the heat, stir in the pasta and all the reserved pasta cooking water, then let it bubble away for a couple of minutes, until the sauce is nice and thick and clinging to the pasta. Spoon into bowls and add a little salt and pepper if you wish.

Sesame noodles with spicy fried "meat"

I ate something similar at my friend Ben Adamo's and loved it. You can make all the elements ahead of time without too much fuss (with the exception of boiling the noodles), making this a great cook-ahead meal for friends.

NOTE Both Chinkiang black vinegar and chilli crisp (I like the Lao Gan Ma brand) can be bought in your nearest East Asian supermarket or online (p 310). You don't need to soak the textured soy protein (TSP) before using. You'll need a pestle and mortar to grind the peppercorns.

SERVES 4

sesame sauce
⅓ vegetable bouillon cube
½ cup tahini
3½ tbsp chilli crisp
2½ tbsp light soy sauce
4 tsp rice vinegar
4 tsp Chinkiang vinegar
¼ tsp Sichuan peppercorns, *ground with a pestle and mortar*

spicy fried ground "meat"
¼ cup canola oil
4 cloves of garlic, *crushed*
¾ x ¾ inch ginger, *grated*
3½ oz textured soy protein (TSP)
1½ tbsp light soy sauce
2½ tbsp hoisin sauce
1½ tbsp Chinkiang vinegar
1 tbsp chilli crisp

noodles
12 oz ramen noodles
8½ oz baby spinach
2 scallions, *finely sliced*

First make the sesame sauce. Crumble the ⅓ bouillon cube into a small saucepan, pour over ⅔ cup of freshly boiled water and stir to dissolve. Add the rest of the sauce ingredients and stir, then leave to one side.

To make the ground "meat," put the oil into a large nonstick frying pan over a medium heat and, when hot, add the garlic and ginger, fry for a minute, then add the TSP. Stir to mix, and cook, stirring frequently (it may catch otherwise), for 4 minutes, or until the TSP turns a roasted almond color. Add ¾ cup of water, the soy sauce, hoisin sauce, Chinkiang vinegar and chilli crisp, then cook for a further 5 minutes, until the water has evaporated and the TSP is dry. Take off the heat, cover with a lid and leave to one side.

Just before serving, bring a large pot to a boil and cook the noodles according to the package instructions. Using tongs or a slotted spoon, transfer the noodles into a colander. Add the spinach to the boiling water, stir to cover the leaves and wilt them, then drain into the colander with the noodles.

Place the sesame sauce over a medium heat, stir and bring to a brief boil, then take off the heat.

To assemble, divide the noodles between four bowls (a fancy way to do this is to take a fork, twizzle the noodles around it to make a little nest, then gently place the nest in the bowl and pull out the fork). Top with a quarter of the spinach, the sauce and a few spoonfuls of the ground "meat," and decorate with the scallions.

Spinach and corn saag

Usually I cook *then* freeze, but this meal has defied the flow chart in that it is an un-freeze *then* cook number. And more surprising still is it's no worse off for it; in fact, I think that frozen spinach makes for better and more delicious saag than fresh does, because the leaves break down into soft and rich buttery greens more easily and without a fight.

NOTE You'll need a blender. The kasoori methi (dried fenugreek leaves) give the saag an unmistakable earthy flavor and can be found in your local South Asian supermarket.

SERVES 4

¼ cup unsalted butter, *plus 2 tbsp to finish*

1 tbsp canola oil

½ tsp cumin seeds

1 red onion, *finely chopped*

3 green finger (or serrano) chillies, *finely chopped*

3 cloves of garlic, *crushed*

2 tbsp kasoori methi

½ tsp ground turmeric

2 tsp salt

2 cups corn niblets, *frozen and thawed, or canned and drained*

1½ lbs frozen spinach, *thawed and drained*

store-bought or homemade naan *(p 306), to serve*

Put the butter and oil into a large saucepan over a medium to high heat. When the butter foams, add the cumin seeds and stir for 30 seconds, then add the onion. Cook for 6 minutes, until soft and translucent, then add the chillies and garlic, and cook for another 2 minutes, until the garlic no longer smells raw. Add the kasoori methi, turmeric and salt, stir to mix, then add the corn and stir again. Finally, add the spinach and 2½ cups of water, and bring to a boil. As soon as it's come to a boil, turn the heat down and simmer for 5 minutes, then take off the heat.

You can either take out a third of the mixture and use a blender to blend it until smooth, then scrape it back into the pan, or you can use an immersion blender and whiz a third of the mixture in the pan. Add the remaining butter and simmer over a medium heat for a final 5 minutes, then serve with hot, buttered naan.

GFO (WITH GF NAAN)   PREP 10 mins / COOK 25 mins

Kimchi and tofu dumplings

When I was due to give birth to my baby, a wise woman gave me some sage advice: "Head to your local Chinese supermarket and pick up some frozen dumplings." Frozen dumplings are a gift to all tired parents everywhere, but the next best gift is making your own and freezing them for a rainy day.

NOTE You'll need a food processor. You can find gyoza wrappers in larger supermarkets and most East Asian supermarkets, but check the label to make sure they're suitable for vegans.

SERVES 2–4
(makes 30 dumplings)

dipping sauce
¼ cup light soy sauce
¼ cup rice vinegar
2 tbsp white wine vinegar
¾ x ¾ inch ginger, *finely grated*

dumplings
10 oz extra-firm tofu, *drained*
8½ oz good-quality vegan kimchi
canola oil
8 scallions, *finely chopped*
salt
30 gyoza (or wonton) wrappers,
  thawed
toasted black sesame seeds, *to
  serve*

To make the dipping sauce, mix all the sauce ingredients in a small bowl, then leave to one side.

Cut the tofu into large pieces and put into a food processor. Weigh out the kimchi – both cabbage and juice – add to the tofu, then blitz until the mixture resembles ground meat. Heat a tablespoon of oil in a nonstick frying pan for which you have a lid, over a medium heat. When hot, add all but a small handful of the scallions. Stir-fry for 4 to 5 minutes, then add the kimchi and tofu mixture and cook for 10 minutes, or until the water disappears. Taste it: you may need to add up to a teaspoon of salt, depending on your kimchi, so add it bit by bit. Tip the mixture into a bowl, and wipe out the frying pan.

To assemble the dumplings, fill a small bowl with water. Take a gyoza wrapper (cover the rest with a damp kitchen towel). Dip a finger in the water bowl and wet the inside edge of the wrapper. Put 2 heaping teaspoons of filling in the center of the wrapper. Fold over the wrapper to enclose the filling, then seal by pressing, pinching or pleating closed, working from one side to the other, pressing out air as you go. Repeat with the remaining wrappers and filling.

To cook, heat a tablespoon of oil in the frying pan over a low heat. When hot, add as many dumplings as will fit in a single layer and fry for a minute or two, until their bottoms are golden. Gently flip, turn down the heat, add 5 tablespoons of water and cover the pan with a lid. Steam for 6 to 7 minutes, until the pastry is soft and the water has evaporated. Repeat with the remaining dumplings.

Throw the reserved scallions into the dipping sauce and pour into smaller serving bowls. Arrange the dumplings on plates, sprinkle with sesame seeds and serve with chopsticks and the dipping sauce.

Pictured overleaf

Spicy tofu nuggets

When you're in the mood, is there anything better than a bucketful of nugs and some coleslaw? Obviously, if your answer is yes, be my guest and move on. But if you're still here, welcome. You, me, my friend the talented cook Milli Taylor, and Snoop Dogg, are all part of a secret gang who hold a fundamental belief: that crushed potato chips make a great shortcut to creating homemade oven-baked crispy things.

NOTE The sauce is quite spicy. For the spice-averse, the nuggets can be served with the sauce on the side (or with ketchup). Gochugaru are Korean chilli flakes; they can be found in East Asian grocery stores and online (p 310). Best served with coleslaw cut with chives.

SERVES 2

nuggets
16 oz extra-firm tofu
½ cup cornstarch
1 tsp baking powder
1 tsp salt
1 tsp ground white pepper
1 tsp garlic granules
1 tsp gochugaru flakes
7 tbsp whole oat milk
5 oz salted chips

gochujang sauce
¼ cup soft light brown sugar
3 tbsp light soy sauce
1 tbsp cider vinegar
¼ cup tomato ketchup
2 tbsp gochujang paste
1½ tbsp toasted sesame seeds, *plus extra to serve*

Preheat the oven to 425°F. Line a large baking sheet (16 x 12 inches) with parchment paper.

Unwrap the tofu from its package and remove as much moisture as possible using paper towel. Using your hands, break the tofu into uneven, craggy, bite-size nuggets (no larger than 1½ inches at the widest point) and put to one side.

To make the batter, put the cornstarch, baking powder, salt, white pepper, garlic granules, gochugaru flakes and oat milk into a large mixing bowl and whisk well until smooth. Next, smash the chips up into really tiny pieces. You can do this in two ways: either put them into a food processor and pulse, or snip a small corner of the bag to let the air out and then roll over it a few times with a rolling pin. Then empty the chips out into a wide, shallow lipped bowl.

Set up a coating station. You'll need the tofu, the cornstarch batter, the bowl of chips and the baking sheet.

Place the tofu pieces in the mixing bowl of batter and coat using a spoon or your hands. Then, piece by piece, shake off any excess and roll around to coat in the chips. Place on the baking sheet and bake for 25 minutes, until crisp and golden.

While the tofu is baking, make the gochujang sauce. Place the sugar, soy sauce, vinegar, ketchup and gochujang in a small pan and whisk to mix. Heat over a medium heat until just bubbling, then take off the heat and stir through the sesame seeds.

If you like it spicy, toss the tofu nuggets through the sauce and pile them high on a plate. Otherwise, judiciously drizzle the sauce over the nuggets, then sprinkle with more sesame seeds.

Tomatoes and other fruit

Tomato and tofu stir-fry with sesame rice

This was intended to be a riff on a Chinese home cook's favorite, egg and tomato stir-fry, which I love as a quick, simple meal. But after replacing the egg with tofu, my world was forever changed. The obvious difference is that it's even quicker and simpler to use tofu instead of the omelet used in the traditional recipe. But tofu's craggy texture works so well here, seamlessly playing along with the richness of the savory, sesame-flavored tomatoes, that there's no going back for me. I'm on Team Tomato with Tofu through and through.

NOTE You'll need a potato masher to mash the tofu.

SERVES 2

1 cup jasmine rice
1 tbsp toasted sesame oil
salt
canola oil
6 scallions, *trimmed, white parts sliced, greens cut on an angle into 1-inch lengths*
10 oz extra-firm tofu, *drained and torn into pieces*
1 lb vine tomatoes, *cut into 8 wedges*
2 cloves of garlic, *crushed*
½ tbsp white miso paste
2½ tbsp light soy sauce
toasted black sesame seeds, *to garnish*

Put the rice into a sieve, rinse really well under the cold tap until the water runs clear, then drain and tip into a medium-sized saucepan for which you have a tight-fitting lid. Add the sesame oil and ½ teaspoon of salt, then add 1½ cups of just-boiled water and bring to a boil. Pop the lid on, turn down the heat to a whisper and leave to simmer for 12 minutes. Turn off the heat and leave to rest – don't be tempted to lift the lid.

Meanwhile, put a plate by the side of the stove, ready for the tofu when it's cooked, and fill a cup with 7 tablespoons of cold water. Put 2 tablespoons of oil into a large frying pan over a medium heat and, once hot, add the scallion greens and ¼ teaspoon of salt, and stir for a minute, until the scallions turn neon green. Add the tofu, mash with a potato masher until it resembles scrambled eggs, then cook, stirring, for 3 minutes, until hot, and spoon out onto the plate.

Wipe out the pan with paper towel and pour in another tablespoon of oil. When that's very hot, add the tomato wedges and leave to cook for 5 minutes, stirring only once – you don't want to break up their shape. Add the garlic and scallion whites, gently stir and cook for another minute. Follow with the miso, soy sauce and the cup of water, stir gently and leave to bubble fiercely for 3 minutes. Finally, return the tofu and scallion greens to the pan, leave to simmer and bubble for 5 minutes, then take off the heat.

Either serve in the pan or transfer to a shallow bowl. Scoop the rice into another bowl and garnish with sesame seeds.

Tomatoes and other fruit

Pineapple fried rice

1980s Britain saw the cultural downgrade of the pineapple. Between "the Man from Del Monte" adverts and cheese-and-pineapple hedgehogs at children's parties it became an object of fun. Thankfully, the good people of Thailand did not bear witness to this and gave it a rightful place in the dinner canon in the form of this fried-rice dish, *khao pad sapparod.*

NOTE Check if the fruit is ripe by pulling a spine from the center of the crown; if it comes out easily, it's ripe. Lee Kum Kee makes a great mushroom vegetarian stir-fry sauce that can be found in larger or East Asian supermarkets.

SERVES 2, generously

3 cups leftover cooked rice or
   1 cup raw jasmine rice
canola oil
⅓ cup roasted unsalted cashews
8 scallions, *finely chopped*
½ tsp salt, *or to taste*
¾ x ¾ inch ginger, *grated*
4 cloves of garlic, *crushed*
2 bird's-eye chillies, *finely chopped*
8½ oz fresh pineapple flesh, *diced*
8½ oz green beans, *topped*
5 oz water chestnuts, *drained*
1 tbsp mild curry powder
3 tbsp mushroom vegetarian
   stir-fry sauce
3 tbsp light soy sauce

to serve
a big handful of fresh Thai basil
   leaves
optional: 1 bird's-eye chilli, *finely
   chopped*
1 lime, *cut into wedges*

If you're cooking the rice from scratch, put the jasmine rice into a sieve and wash really well under the cold tap until the water runs clear. Drain and put into a saucepan for which you have a tight-fitting lid. Cover with 1½ cups of freshly boiled water, bring to a boil, then pop the lid on and simmer for 12 minutes. Take off the heat and leave, covered, to steam for 5 minutes. Spread the cooked rice on a large plate and leave to cool to room temperature.

Put a tablespoon of oil into a wide frying pan for which you have a lid and set it over a medium heat. When the oil is hot, add the cashews and fry, stirring, for a few minutes, until golden, then scoop out onto a plate. Put another 2 tablespoons of oil into the same pan and, when hot, add the scallions and ½ teaspoon of salt, and fry, stirring, for 3 minutes, until soft and neon green. Add the ginger, garlic and chillies, stir-fry for 2 minutes, then stir in the pineapple and fry for a minute. Add the green beans and the water chestnuts, mix well, then cover the pan and leave to cook for 5 or so minutes, until the beans are bendy; if the mixture starts to stick and the beans are not yet soft, add a splash of water to the pan.

Stir in the curry powder, then pour in the stir-fry sauce and soy sauce, and cook for couple of minutes. Add the cooked rice and mix in gently. Turn up the heat to high and fry hard for 5 minutes, turning halfway through. When piping hot, turn out onto a platter, scatter over the Thai basil leaves, fried cashews, and more chilli if you wish, and serve with lime wedges alongside.

Summer vegetable achari

In August the great British corn harvest starts, leaving farmers' markets and supermarkets groaning with primary-yellow batons. I've been experimenting with different ways of using them, and this curry is the result. It's the lovechild of a Gujarati corn curry (*makai nu shaak*), with its fresh tomatoes, and a Punjabi achari "pickled" curry, which employs big, hot, salty and sour flavors that the corn, with its natural sweetness, slots right into.

NOTE If you can't get your hands on fresh corn cobs, use frozen kernels – they're often half the price of (and taste more natural than) their canned counterparts.

SERVES 4

10 oz runner beans
5 tbsp canola oil
½ tsp fennel seeds
½ tsp cumin seeds
1 tsp black mustard seeds
¼ tsp fenugreek seeds
1 tsp nigella seeds
3 corn cobs, *kernels sliced, to get 12 oz*
3 cloves of garlic, *crushed*
1 red onion, *halved and thinly sliced*
1½ lbs mixed tomatoes, *chopped – vine tomatoes quartered, cherries halved, big ones cut into wedges*
1 tsp Kashmiri chilli powder
1¼ tsp salt
chapattis or naan *(pp 306–7), to serve*

First prepare the runner beans. Remove the tough strings by running a vegetable peeler down the sides of the beans. Top, tail and finely slice the beans at a steep angle, and keep to one side.

Put the oil into a wide frying pan over a medium heat and wait until it is properly hot (put a wooden spoon into the oil: if bubbles form around it, it's ready). When hot, add the fennel, cumin, black mustard, fenugreek and nigella seeds, and leave them to sizzle for 30 seconds. Add the runner beans and corn kernels, and fry, stirring, for 3 to 4 minutes, then add the garlic and onion, and fry for 5 minutes more.

Tip the tomatoes into the pan, stir in the chilli powder and salt, then cook for about 10 minutes, until the tomatoes are starting to break down and letting out their juices, but are still just clinging on to their shape. Taste, adjust the seasoning if need be, and serve with chapattis or naan.

V/GFO (WITH GF BREAD)   PREP 10 mins / COOK 25 mins

Mango and paneer curry

At the start of mango season, my grandfather Madhuradas would drive down to Paul's Fruit and Veg, a wholesale distributor in Leicester, and buy a box of mangoes for everyone he loved. It's been 27 years since he passed away, but I still end up buying too many in the brief season and this is a great way of using them.

NOTE Look for mangoes that are smooth-skinned, wrinkle-free and tender. Fresh curry leaves can be found in large supermarkets, Indian supermarkets and online (p 310). Freeze any leftover leaves for another time.

SERVES 4

2 large mangoes (2 lbs)
canola oil
1 lb hard paneer, *cut into
   1-inch cubes*
16 fresh curry leaves
1 tsp black mustard seeds
1 large yellow onion, *halved and
   thinly sliced*
¾ x ¾ inch ginger, *grated*
2 cloves of garlic, *crushed*
2 green finger (or serrano) chillies,
   finely chopped
1 tbsp ground coriander
¾ tsp ground turmeric
1¼ tsp salt
½ tsp superfine sugar
1 x 14-oz can of coconut milk

cooked basmati rice *(p 305),
   to serve*

To prepare the mangoes, peel them, then slice off a fat "cheek" from one side of each fruit, keeping the knife as close to the stone as possible. Repeat on the other side, then cut off the two ends, salvaging as much flesh from the stone as possible, and cut the flesh into ¾-inch-square pieces (keep the stones to nibble on as a cook's perk). If your mangoes are too soft to peel, cut them first, then score the flesh into ¾-inch cubes with a knife and use a large spoon to scoop out the flesh.

Place a plate to one side of the stove. Put a tablespoon of oil into a wide nonstick frying pan over a medium heat and fry the paneer for 5 to 6 minutes, turning every piece with a spatula until golden brown. Transfer to the plate and leave to one side.

To the same pan, add 2 more tablespoons of oil and, when really hot, add the curry leaves. Let them crackle and crisp, then transfer half of them to the paneer plate. Add the mustard seeds to the pan with the remaining curry leaves, let the seeds pop for a few seconds, then add the onion. Cook for 8 minutes, stirring occasionally, until golden and starting to brown, then add the ginger, garlic and chillies. Cook for 2 minutes, then add the coriander, turmeric, salt and sugar, and stir to mix.

Add the mango pieces, along with ¾ cup of water, bring the mixture to a bubble, and simmer for 8 minutes, until soft and the water has nearly all gone. Then put the paneer back into the pan along with the coconut milk, bring to a simmer, and cook for another 5 minutes. Take off the heat, taste, and adjust the seasoning if need be.

Either serve in the pan, or transfer to a large bowl and scatter over the reserved curry leaves, with freshly steamed basmati rice alongside.

GF PREP 5 mins / COOK 40 mins

Tomatoes and other fruit

MJJ cold noodles

A celebration of May, June and July, the months in which tomatoes and mangoes overlap.

NOTE Tofu puffs are a joy: they're spongy, chewy and soak up any flavors they encounter. They can be found in East Asian supermarkets and online (p 310).

SERVES 2 with leftovers

1 big ripe mango, *peeled and cut into ½-inch dice*

5 oz ripe tomatoes, *sliced into wedges*

8 tofu puffs, *quartered*

1 lime, *zested and quartered*

¼ cup canola oil

3 cloves of garlic, *crushed*

2 stalks of lemongrass, *outer leaves and top third discarded, the rest finely chopped*

1 bird's-eye chilli, *very finely chopped*

1½ tsp superfine sugar

4 tbsp rice vinegar

¾ tsp salt

3 tbsp store-bought crispy fried onions, *plus 3 tbsp to finish*

7 oz soba noodles

½ oz fresh Thai basil or fresh ordinary basil, *leaves picked*

Place the mango, tomatoes, tofu puffs and lime zest in a large bowl, mix and leave to one side.

To make the dressing, heat the oil in a small saucepan and, when hot, add the garlic, lemongrass and chilli. Cook for 2 minutes, or until the garlic turns golden brown, then take off the heat and add the sugar, vinegar, salt and 3 tablespoons of the crispy fried onions. Leave to one side to cool.

Boil the noodles, according to the package instructions, then drain and rinse in a sieve under the cold tap until the noodles are cold. Drain again really well, then put the noodles, dressing and basil leaves into the bowl and mix everything gently together (I like to use my hands). Tip out onto a platter or into bowls and top with the remaining crispy fried onions. Serve with the wedges of lime.

Marmite risotto with tomato and crispy chilli butter

Some people have big epiphanies, but not me. I had two small ones though. The first was that I don't like the taste of vegetable stock: use too much and there's no return. This led to my second illuminating discovery, namely that Marmite makes great stock and, well, here we are. This risotto, contrary to what you might assume, is very gentle (the Marmite is a back note); the party is in the tomato and chilli butter, in which I've used my favorite chilli crisp to give the cherry tomatoes some fireworks.

NOTE Any chilli crisp would work, but my favorite, by Lao Gan Ma, can be found in larger supermarkets, as well as in Chinese grocery stores and online (p 310).

SERVES 4

chilli butter

1¼ lbs cherry tomatoes, *halved*

2 tbsp extra virgin olive oil

½ tsp salt

¼ cup unsalted butter, *vegan or dairy*

2 tbsp chilli crisp sediment

risotto

¼ cup unsalted butter, *vegan or dairy*

2 tbsp extra virgin olive oil

1 large yellow onion, *finely chopped*

1 tsp salt

3 cloves of garlic, *crushed*

1¾ cups arborio rice

¾ cup dry white wine

4 tsp Marmite, *dissolved in 4½ cups boiled water*

Preheat the oven to 400°F and line a baking sheet with parchment paper.

Put the tomatoes for the chilli butter on the baking sheet, coat with the olive oil and sprinkle over the salt. Bake for 35 minutes, turning once halfway, until sticky and browning (but not burnt). Remove and leave to cool.

Now for the risotto. Put 2 tablespoons of the butter and all the olive oil into a medium-sized pan set over a medium heat, then add the onion and a teaspoon of salt, and fry, stirring regularly, for 8 minutes, until soft, translucent and golden. Add the garlic, cook for a further 2 minutes, then add the rice and stir to coat. Pour in the wine, let it sizzle away, then add a ladleful of Marmite stock. Cook, stirring gently and regularly, until the stock is absorbed by the rice, then add another ladle of stock to the pan and repeat. Carry on cooking and adding stock as necessary, until the rice is tender and the risotto very creamy (rather than too stiff or too loose), which may take up to 30 minutes (if you run out of stock, add some hot water instead). Take off the heat and stir through the remaining 2 tablespoons of butter.

To make the chilli butter, heat the butter and chilli crisp sediment in a small saucepan and, when the butter has melted, mix in the tomatoes and take off the heat. To serve, dollop the risotto into shallow bowls and put a couple of spoonfuls of the tomato chilli butter in the center of each portion.

Tomato and lemongrass pot noodles

"A pot noodle with a touch of class" is how a subeditor described this recipe when it was published in the *Guardian*, and I'm inclined to agree. I wrote it in homage to a Martha Stewart technique, a revelation, in which she made a one-pot spaghetti by putting all the ingredients – the sauce, pasta and cooking water – in the same pan and what emerged 9 minutes later was a perfectly cooked meal. Genius.

NOTE I use a Nutribullet to make the paste, but you could use a hand blender.

SERVES 2

1 x 1 inch ginger, *roughly chopped*
4 cloves of garlic, *roughly chopped*
3 stalks of lemongrass, *outer leaves and top third discarded, the rest roughly chopped*
¾ oz fresh cilantro stems and leaves, *chopped*
2 bird's-eye chillies, *roughly chopped*
¼ cup canola oil
14 oz baby plum tomatoes, *halved*
1 x 14-oz can of coconut milk
1¼ tsp salt
7 oz soba noodles
¾ oz fresh Thai basil leaves, *leaves picked*

Throw the first six ingredients into a blender and blitz to a paste. Set a wide pan for which you have a lid on a medium heat and, once hot, add the paste and cook, stirring, for 3 to 4 minutes, until it releases its oils into the pan.

Stir in the tomatoes, pop the lid on and cook, stirring only occasionally so as not to break them up, for 5 to 6 minutes, until they collapse, go soft and become a little jammy.

Pour in the coconut milk, then fill up the empty can 1½ times with water and add that to the pan, too. Gently stir in the salt, then bring the mixture to a boil. Drop in the noodles, so they're submerged, leave to bubble away for about 5 minutes, until tender, then stir through the Thai basil. Either serve in the pan or, if you're feeling fancy, distribute between two bowls: ladle in the sauce and twirl the noodles into the bowls using a fork.

Lima beans with rose harissa and dill

I went through a period of wanting to be a *flâneur*, which affected my cooking as I preferred my effort-to-reward ratio to be skewed heavily in favor of the reward. Ergo these brothy, spiced, tomato-ey beans that practically cook themselves. If you're feeling lazy, eat them just as they are (preferably in the garden with a baguette and cold wine) or, to step things up, break open some jarred artichokes and whip out the good flatbreads, a salad and some hummus, for a picky-bits, meze-style meal.

NOTE Some harissa spice blends include salt, like the one I use made by Bart's Spices, while others use little or no salt, so you'll need to adjust the seasoning to taste. Always measure your rose water away from the pan, to stop an accidental overpour.

SERVES 2–4

extra virgin olive oil
6 cloves of garlic, *crushed*
1 fresh red chilli, *finely chopped*
1 lb large ripe vine tomatoes, *grated*
   (skins composted)
1 tbsp harissa spice blend
1 tbsp red wine vinegar
scant ¼ tsp rose water
1½ tbsp sun-dried tomato paste
2 x 15-oz cans of lima beans, *not*
   drained
salt
½ oz fresh dill
2 tbsp lemon juice, *from 1 lemon*
baguette or flatbreads *(pp 305–6),*
   to serve

Heat ¼ cup of oil in a medium-sized saucepan on a medium to high heat and, once it's hot, add the crushed garlic and cook for a minute or two, until the pungent smell disappears and the garlic turns a pale shade of gold.

Add the chilli, cook for another couple of minutes, then add the grated tomatoes, harissa spice blend, vinegar, rose water and sun-dried tomato paste, and let everything bubble away vivaciously for 8 to 10 minutes, until the tomatoes have reduced and the mixture is quite paste-like.

Add the lima beans and the liquid from the cans, mix, then leave to cook away for 10 minutes, until the beans are hot and soft. Add the salt a ¼ teaspoon at a time, until the mix tastes just right to you (I used a teaspoon; you may need more or less).

While the beans are cooking, chop the dill very finely, put it into a small bowl with the lemon juice, 3 tablespoons of oil and ¼ teaspoon of salt, and mix.

Transfer the beans to a serving dish, spoon over the lemon and dill oil and serve with baguette or flatbreads.

Simple tomato dal

A noble use of summer tomatoes.

NOTE Curry leaves can be found in most larger supermarkets and South Asian supermarkets. Freeze what you don't use for another day. You'll need a blender.

SERVES 4

1½ cups split red lentils
1¼ lbs ripe tomatoes, *roughly chopped*
¼ cup canola oil
1 tsp black mustard seeds
10 fresh curry leaves
5 cloves of garlic, *crushed*
¾ x ¾ inch ginger, *finely grated*
2 green finger (or serrano) chillies, *finely chopped, or 1 tsp Kashmiri chilli powder*
1 tsp ground cumin
1 tsp ground turmeric
scant ½ tsp ground black pepper
1¾ tsp salt
cooked basmati rice *(p 305), to serve*

Wash the lentils in a sieve under the cold tap until the water runs clear and leave to drain on one side. Put the chopped tomatoes into a blender and blend until smooth, then set aside.

Put the oil into a large saucepan over a medium heat. When hot, add the mustard seeds and curry leaves, let them crackle and pop for a few seconds (but if they don't, move on with the next step as they'll quickly become bitter), then add the garlic, ginger and chillies. Stir and cook for 2 minutes, until the smell of the garlic goes from raw to cooked, then add the cumin, turmeric, pepper and salt, and stir to mix.

Add the fresh tomato paste, mix, cock a lid over the top and let it cook for 10 minutes, stirring occasionally. Add the lentils and 4 cups of water, stir, cock the lid over the top again and bring to a boil, then turn the heat down and cook for a further 10 to 15 minutes, or until the lentils and water have come together – not merged completely, but have formed a level of uniformity you understand to be dal (rather than lentils in broth, for example).

Serve with steamed basmati rice.

Side

show

Garlic chard

A universal side (in that I can't think of anything it wouldn't go well with).

NOTE I really love the type of chard with thick white stems, partly because it feels like there are two vegetables in one: the juicy, creamy stems and the gently bitter, dark emerald-green leaves. This is a super simple and delightful way to cook them, and it can easily be doubled (however, you'll need to increase the cooking times by a minute or so).

SERVES 4 as a side

14 oz Swiss chard
3 tbsp canola oil
4 cloves of garlic, *crushed*
scant ½ tsp salt

Wash the chard and shake dry. Cut the stems into ¾-inch slices and the leaves into 2½- to 3-inch sections. Keep both in separate piles on the chopping board.

Put the oil into a large frying pan for which you have a lid, over a medium heat. When hot, add the chard stalks, stir, then pop the lid on and cook for 4 minutes, stirring halfway through. Add the garlic, stir to mix, then add the chard leaves, the salt and ¼ cup of water. Stir to mix, pop the lid on again and cook for 5 minutes, stirring once or twice.

To serve, transfer to a serving plate and pour over the pan juices.

Kimchi tofu and carrot salad

Punchy and crunchy and good for a crowd. Good kimchi is key here (p 214) – that and an excellent knife.

NOTE The longer this salad sits, the more juices it will release, so combine everything just before serving. Keep pre-prepared vegetables under a damp towel, put the apple in cold water and keep the blended dressing ready in the fridge.

SERVES 6 as a side

7 oz kimchi, *drained*
5 tbsp canola oil
10 oz extra-firm tofu, *drained*
¼ green cabbage (5 oz)
1 crisp eating apple (I like Braeburn)
2 large carrots (7 oz), *peeled*
3 scallions
¾ oz fresh cilantro, *chopped*
½–1 tsp salt
toasted sesame oil, *to serve*

First make the dressing: put the kimchi and canola oil into a blender and blend until smooth. Next, get yourself a big bowl and your sharpest knife ready for all the chopping.

Pat the tofu dry with paper towel and cut into wafer-thin slices (around ⅛ inch), then stack the slices and cut into thin matchsticks. Pop into the bowl.

Finely shred the cabbage, then chop the apple into matchsticks the same shape and size as the tofu, and do the same with the carrots. Cut the scallions in half, then finely shred lengthways. Put it all into the bowl.

Add the chopped cilantro and mix with clean hands, scrunching a little to wilt the salad. Add ½ teaspoon of salt, mix and taste and, if need be, add the rest, ¼ teaspoon at a time.

Pour over the dressing and mix well, then tip onto a serving plate and drizzle over a few drops of sesame oil.

V/GF   PREP 5 mins / ASSEMBLE 25 mins

Two leafy salads

Summer leaf salad with mint and dill

The only salad you'll ever need (except for the other three salads in this chapter).

NOTE I use pre-bought jarred green "frenk" chillies pickled in brine and vinegar, but any pickled chillies will do. Add as many as you like. This recipe can easily be doubled.

SERVES 4 as a side

**9 oz Baby Gem or romaine lettuce
(4 cups chopped)**
½ oz fresh dill, *leaves picked*
½ oz fresh mint, *leaves picked*
1–2 pickled green chillies,
finely chopped
3 tbsp canola oil
1½ tbsp rice vinegar
¼ tsp salt

Cut the base of the lettuce to release the leaves. Tear the larger ones in two across the belly, and leave the smaller ones intact. When you get to the core, slice it up. Put it all into a large bowl, then add the herbs and chillies, to taste.

In a small bowl, vigorously mix together the oil, vinegar and salt, and dress the salad just before serving. I always, and briefly, use clean hands to do this to coat the leaves, but as you were (there are no rules as such). I like to transfer it all to a shallow bowl to serve.

V/GF   PREP 2 mins / ASSEMBLE 5 mins

Winter leaf salad with miso and ginger

This salad would take issue with being called a side, with the amount of big energy it vibrates. The sweet, fiery ginger dressing is the perfect match for radicchio's bitter leaves.

NOTE There are many varieties of radicchio. The best type for this salad is Chioggia, which is often just called "radicchio" because it's the most commonly available. The rosette-shaped Grumolo variety is also lovely if you can find it. Clearspring make a great and widely available sweet miso.

SERVES 4 as a side

1½ tbsp shiro or sweet white miso
1½ tbsp light agave syrup
¾ x ¾ inch ginger, *finely grated*
3 tbsp canola oil
½ tbsp rice vinegar
¼ tsp salt
**10 oz radicchio (1 head of
Chioggia)**

Whisk the miso, agave, ginger, oil, vinegar and salt together in the bowl you're going to serve the salad in. If it's really thick, add a little water, a teaspoon at a time (I use 3), until roughly the consistency of liquid honey.

Just before serving, cut the base off the radicchio, rip the radicchio leaves into the bowl and toss using clean hands to get the dressing into the leaves.

V/GF   PREP 5 mins / ASSEMBLE 5 mins

Shredded salt and vinegar potato salad

I have an admission to make: I don't love a traditional potato salad, but this is one I can't stop eating. The potatoes should be cooked to just past raw to retain a mere whisper of a crunch.

NOTE You'll need a good nonstick pan with a lid. I use King Edward potatoes, but any other kind of potato is good too. You can prepare the potato matchsticks a few hours ahead of time; just keep them well submerged in cold water until you're ready to cook.

SERVES 4 as a side

4 medium potatoes (1¼ lbs), *peeled*
2 tbsp canola oil
2 scallions, *finely sliced at an angle*
1 tbsp white wine vinegar
1¼ tsp salt
1 tsp toasted sesame oil
½ oz fresh chives, *finely chopped*

Have a large bowl of water to one side. Take the potatoes one by one and cut them into wafer-thin slices. Then lay the slices on top of one another in small batches and cut into matchsticks, as thinly and evenly as you're able. Pop them into the water and repeat with the remaining potatoes. Swish the water around with your hands, then drain the potatoes really, really well, shaking off any excess water. If the potatoes are wet, the oil might spit when you add them to the pan.

Heat the canola oil in a large frying pan and, when smoking hot, add the potatoes. Stir-fry for 3 minutes, then add the scallions, vinegar, salt and sesame oil. Mix, then pop the lid on for a final minute, until the potatoes no longer taste raw, but have a slight crunch to them. If they're still tasting too raw, keep them in the pan for another minute, then take off the heat. Toss through nearly all the chives, then taste and adjust the seasoning if need be.

Serve on a large plate or platter, with the remaining chives scattered over.

Asparagus and cashew thoran

Never has a dish been so maligned when given the name of "side." Here, asparagus is given the classic Keralan treatment of mustard seeds, cashew, coconut and lemon, and it becomes something very special indeed. A side in name, but a star on the table.

NOTE This is great with butter paneer (p 99) or any dal. You can buy fresh curry leaves from most major supermarkets and most Indian grocery stores. Freeze any that you don't use. You will need a pestle and mortar to crush the cumin seeds.

SERVES 4–6 as a side

1½ lbs asparagus, *woody stalks removed*

2 tbsp canola oil

10–15 fresh curry leaves

½ tsp cumin seeds, *crushed with a pestle and mortar*

½ tsp black mustard seeds

1 red onion, *finely chopped*

¾ x ¾ inch ginger, *grated*

1 green finger (or serrano) chilli, *finely chopped*

4 medium-sized ripe tomatoes, *roughly chopped*

a big handful of roasted unsalted cashews

¾ tsp salt

1 tbsp lemon juice, *from ½ lemon*

¼ cup unsweetened shredded

Have all your ingredients ready, because this dish comes together very quickly.

When your ingredients are at hand, cut the asparagus into 1½-inch lengths at a sharp angle. Put the oil into a large frying pan over a high heat and, once it's hot, add the curry leaves, cumin and mustard seeds. Wait up to a minute for them to snap, crackle and pop, then add the onion and fry hard for 5 minutes. Add the ginger and chilli, fry for another 3 minutes, until the mixture is soft and browning, then add the tomatoes, asparagus, cashews and salt, and stir-fry for 4 minutes, or until the asparagus is al dente.

Stir in the lemon juice and coconut, take off the heat, then transfer to a serving plate.

V/GF   PREP 10 mins / COOK 20 mins

Side show

Sesame and lime broccolini

Never not welcome on my table.

NOTE You'll need something to bash the sesame seeds with, like a pestle and mortar or a spice grinder. Use a quality vegan fish sauce (Tofuna makes a good one). This recipe can easily be doubled.

SERVES 4

3 tbsp raw black or white sesame seeds *(or a mix)*
1 tsp soft light brown sugar
¼ tsp salt
10 oz broccolini, *woody ends removed*
1½ tbsp vegan fish sauce
1½ tbsp lime juice, *from 1 lime*

If your sesame seeds aren't roasted already, place a large saucepan (large enough to fit the broccolini in later) over a high heat and dry-fry the seeds for 1 to 2 minutes, until deep golden brown, then transfer immediately to a plate and allow to cool.

Grind the sesame seeds, sugar and salt into fine crumbs with a pestle and mortar or spice grinder and leave to one side.

Fill your large saucepan with water and bring to a boil over a medium heat. Carefully drop the broccolini in and boil for 5½ to 6 minutes, until tender to soft (or beyond crunchy). Drain really well, let steam dry for a minute, then tip into a bowl. Add the sesame-seed mix, the vegan fish sauce and the lime juice, and mix with clean hands until well combined.

V/GF PREP less than 5 mins / COOK 10 mins

Taiwanese-style pickled cucumbers

A simple soy-and-vinegar cucumber pickle that comes together quickly and is incredibly versatile.

NOTE Small, firm cucumbers like baby cucumbers, Lebanese cucumbers or gherkins are best here, as they're less watery. If you use the bigger ones, scoop out the seeds in the center of the cucumber and chop into half-moons.

MAKES a 16-oz jar

8½ oz baby cucumbers, *cut into ½-inch slices*
7 tbsp light soy sauce
¼ cup superfine sugar
5 tbsp white wine vinegar

Wash a 16-oz jar and lid in hot soapy water, rinse well and allow to air dry.

Place all the ingredients in a small to medium-sized saucepan and bring to a boil, then immediately lower the heat and simmer for 5 minutes. Take off the heat and leave to cool, then decant into the clean, dry jar. Store the jar of pickles in the fridge for up to two weeks.

V PREP 5 mins / COOK 10 mins (plus cooling time)

Turnip cake

This turnip cake is based on a classic dim sum. Sometimes called radish cake, it is confusingly made with daikon radish. It's one of my favorites, ticking a lot of my boxes: it's sweet and savory, near custardy in the middle, but crisp on the outside. You can serve it with drinks as a starter (I have), but it makes for a lavish side; try it with the roasted eggplant with silken tofu on p 33 or with Ben Benton strikes again (p 36).

NOTE   You'll need Thai rice flour – not the glutinous variety – to make this. It is much finer than supermarket rice flour. You'll also need a 4-cup ovenproof dish (ceramic, glass, or even a foil takeout container), and a bigger ovenproof dish, in which to put the 4-cup container. To get ahead, make the day before and fry before serving.

SERVES 6 as a side

turnip cake
canola oil
scant 1 cup Thai rice flour
    (non-glutinous)
1 tbsp cornstarch
1½ tsp superfine sugar
1¼ tsp salt
6 large shallots (7 oz net), *halved
    and thinly sliced*
4½ oz fresh shiitake mushrooms,
    diced
2 cloves of garlic, *crushed*
1 large daikon radish (14 oz),
    coarsely grated

sauce
3 tbsp dark soy sauce
2 tbsp light agave syrup
1 tbsp toasted sesame oil
1 tsp white wine vinegar

3 scallions, *finely sliced,
    to serve*

First, lightly oil the ovenproof dish you're going to use for the turnip cake and preheat the oven to 475°F.

Next, make the batter. Put the flour, cornstarch, sugar and salt into a bowl, pour in ¾ cup + 3 tablespoons of water, stir and leave to one side.

Put 2½ tablespoons of oil into a large frying pan over a medium heat and, when hot, add the shallots and the mushrooms and cook for 8 minutes, until soft and threatening to caramelize. Add the garlic, cook for 2 minutes, then add the grated daikon. Cook for 10 to 12 minutes, stirring regularly, until the water has evaporated and the mixture is looking quite dry. Scoop the mixture into the batter and mix, then pour it into your oiled ovenproof dish.

Fill and boil the kettle. Tightly cover the dish with foil, sealing it well around the edges so that no air can escape. Put your bigger baking dish into the hot oven, then put the smaller container (with its foil lid) inside the bigger one. Carefully pour the water from the kettle into the bigger dish to come about halfway up the side of the smaller dish. Bake for 40 minutes, then carefully remove the turnip cake and set aside to cool. Allow the water in the other baking dish to cool before you pour it away. Remove the foil lid from the cake, let it cool, cover, then transfer to the fridge for an hour, or overnight, until cold.

Just before serving, make the sauce. Put the soy sauce, agave syrup, sesame oil and vinegar into a small bowl and mix, then leave to one side.

Cut the turnip cake into twelve equal slices. Put a tablespoon of oil into your frying pan, add six slices of turnip cake, fry for 3 minutes on each side until golden brown, then transfer to a serving plate. Repeat with the remaining slices. To serve, spoon over a little of the sauce (serve the rest on the side) and sprinkle over the scallions.

V   PREP 15 mins / COOK 1 hr 30 mins (plus cooling time)

Side show

Golden coin eggs

Spicy little treasures, straight out of Hunan. They're particularly good with simple rice dishes.

NOTE Make sure you do all the prep up front, as this dish comes together very quickly. You'll need dried fermented soybeans called "salted black beans," which you can find in your local Chinese shop or online (p 310). To get gently curled slices of scallion like those in the photo, pop them into a bowl of cold water just after cutting, until needed.

SERVES 4 as a side

5 tbsp cornstarch
4 large eggs
¼ cup canola oil
¾ x ¾ inch ginger, *finely grated*
3 cloves of garlic, *crushed*
1 tsp chilli flakes
1 tbsp salted black beans, *rinsed and chopped*
4 scallions, *3 finely sliced, 1 cut into long, thin strips*
1½ tbsp light soy sauce
1½ tbsp Shaoxing wine

Prepare a bowl of very cold water, throw some ice cubes in there for good measure if you like, and leave to one side. Tip the cornstarch into a shallow lipped bowl and leave this to one side too.

Bring a medium-sized pan of water to a boil and carefully lower in the eggs. Reduce the heat to a simmer and boil for 9 minutes. Drain the eggs and lower into the cold water. Crack them on the bottom of the bowl to let some water in between the egg and shell, leave for 2 minutes, then peel.

Using a wet knife, chop the eggs into ½-inch rings, wiping down the knife when needed to get clean slices. Place the slices on the cornstarch plate and gently coat with the cornstarch using a teaspoon.

With all the ingredients prepared and to the side of the stove, heat the oil in a wide nonstick frying pan over a medium heat until very hot. Using your fingers, quickly and carefully lower the egg slices, one by one, into the oil, shaking off any excess cornstarch. Fry for around 2 to 2½ minutes on each side, until golden, then add the ginger, garlic, chilli flakes, black beans and the 3 finely sliced scallions. Stir-fry for around 30 seconds, then add the soy sauce and Shaoxing wine. Stir-fry for another 30 seconds, then take off the heat. Shuffle out the eggs onto a serving plate and top with the remaining scallion.

Thai tomato and zucchini salad

From the first bite, the som tam hit me from all angles. It was cold and crunchy, but also hot, sour, salty and sweet, which was exactly perfect for the 100-degree Thai heat. It's not particularly easy to find unripe papaya here, so this recipe uses zucchini and tomatoes instead – a taste of Bangkok, but via an English allotment. Serve cold, with an even colder Thai beer.

NOTE The longer this salad sits, the more juice the zucchini will release, so unless eating straight away, serve with tongs, then spoon over the juices and sprinkle over the breadcrumbs when serving. Julienning the zucchini is infinitely easier with a julienne peeler. You'll need a blender or a pestle and mortar.

SERVES 4 as a side

dressing
3 bird's-eye chillies
3 cloves of garlic, *roughly chopped*
3½ tbsp light soy sauce
¼ cup lime juice, *from 3 limes*
canola oil
1½ tsp palm or soft light
    brown sugar

salad
1 lb cherry tomatoes, *halved*
2 zucchini (14 oz), *julienned*
a large handful (½ oz) of fresh
    Thai basil leaves, *shredded*
heaping ¼ cup salted peanuts,
    crushed
¼ cup unseasoned dried
    breadcrumbs
¼ tsp salt

First make the dressing. Roughly chop 2 chillies and put them into a blender with the garlic, soy sauce, lime juice, 2 tablespoons of oil and the sugar, and whizz until well blended. Alternatively, pound the chillies and garlic to a paste with a pestle and mortar, add the liquids and sugar, and mix.

Put the tomato halves into a large bowl, then lightly squash them with your hand. Pour over the dressing and set aside. Put the julienned zucchini on top of the tomatoes, but don't mix them in just yet. Sprinkle over the shredded basil.

Now for the peanut breadcrumbs. Put 2 tablespoons of oil into a frying pan over a medium heat. While it's warming up, very finely chop the remaining chilli. When the oil is hot, add the chilli, peanuts, breadcrumbs and salt, stir for around 4 minutes, until golden brown, then take off the heat.

To assemble the salad, mix the zucchini and basil into the tomatoes, then tip out onto a lipped platter. Scatter the breadcrumbs on top at the last minute, or wait until people have helped themselves and encourage them to sprinkle a small mountain over their own serving.

The kitchen gods

Every Hindu kitchen has a god perched on a shelf, sitting in the spice cupboard or presiding over the microwave.

When Hugh and I bought our first home, the big moment wasn't when we went to collect the keys from the estate agent. It was when my parents came over to do the *navi ghar ni puja*, or new house prayer. Despite us not being hugely religious, this prayer was meant to bring light, positivity and good energy into the space, and it was hard to say no to that, especially because we'd moved into an area infamous, at the time, for stabbings and drug raids.

Mum laid a copper tray on the floor in which she placed a red and gold lametta cloth. She unwrapped two A-lister gods, Ganesh, the elephant god and the remover of obstacles, and Lakshmi, the goddess of prosperity, and placed them at the back of the tray where they could oversee our offerings. These offerings did not seem to have caught up with modern times. There were no Wagon Wheels or Pringles, but instead a series of time-tested bowls of unbroken basmati rice, mung beans, some coins, flowers and incense. She lit the incense and said a few words, brushed each of our foreheads with a bright red powder made using turmeric and slaked lime, then turned her attention to the stove. She placed a small saucepan of milk on it and allowed it to boil over, which is an invitation from the house for abundance and prosperity. The mung beans were transferred to a small plastic bag, and Mum told me to cook them for guests who came to the house. I never cooked them: the blessed beans felt far too sacred. I found them years later and planted them in the garden, hoping they might, like Jack's beanstalk, turn into something magical to reassure me I hadn't forsaken the gods. We had a good crop of runner beans that year: a consolation prize.

Ganesh and Lakshmi have remained in the kitchen; next to them is Annapurna, the Hindu goddess of nourishment, who holds a spoon in her hands. My last trip to Mumbai yielded a miniature Buddha, who I presumed might be encouraging in my cooking endeavors due to his round belly. From time to time, I offer them blossoms, the occasional piece of fruit, and small, shiny craft gems that my little girls like to keep in their pockets.

The more I thought about my kitchen gods, and spent time in friends' kitchens, the more I realized that everyone has their own kitchen-based talismans, objects that represent happiness and reassurance, whether it's their grandma's old recipe book or a mum's Sunday-best platter, photos tacked to the fridge, their children's artwork or magnets from holidays past. It's not the gods per se that are important, it's the feeling they give and what they speak for.

Mine give me the same feeling that my mother's wooden spoon does, or the small copper pot my grandma gifted to me: whether by connection, tradition or ritual, the comfort and joy that I am – and all of us are – never cooking alone in the kitchen.

Happy

endings

Tahini banana bread

Creating a recipe for a vegan and gluten-free banana bread was my Mount Everest. Taking out wheat flour, dairy and eggs from traditional cake baking left me with just bananas and sugar. But thanks to the know-how of Freddie Janssen of Snackbar (whose vegan tahini banana bread is excellent) and a generous online community who recommended buckwheat flour, plus seven rounds of testing, I finally arrived at a recipe that, personally, I cannot keep my hands off.

NOTE You'll need a 2-pound loaf pan. If you're gluten intolerant, check the oat milk is gluten-free.

MAKES a 1kg loaf

canola oil
1²/₃ **cups buckwheat flour**
1½ **tbsp milled flaxseed**
1 **tsp baking powder**
¾ **tsp baking soda**
¾ **tsp salt**
6 **bananas:** *5 peeled to get 14 oz flesh*
⅓ **cup tahini**
1 **cup soft light brown sugar**
1½ **tsp apple cider vinegar**
1 **tbsp pure vanilla extract**
¾ **cup + 5 tsp whole oat milk**
1 **tbsp demerara sugar**
unsalted dairy-free butter, *to serve*

Preheat the oven to 400°F. Line a 2-lb loaf pan with parchment paper, making sure some hangs over the edges, and grease the sides with a little oil.

Put the buckwheat flour, flaxseed, baking powder, baking soda and salt into a large bowl and whisk to distribute everything evenly.

In another bowl, use a fork to mash the 14 oz of bananas to a paste, then add the tahini, soft light brown sugar, vinegar, vanilla, oat milk and 2 tablespoons of oil. Mix well, then scrape into the flour bowl and mix until the batter is smooth and uniform.

Pour into the lined pan, then tap it on a worktop or table to level out the surface and release any air bubbles. Slice the remaining banana in half lengthways and gently press cut side up into the batter. Sprinkle over the demerara sugar.

Bake for 30 minutes, then turn the pan around and lower the heat to 350°F. Bake for a further 30 minutes, until the top is golden and a skewer comes out clean, then take out of the oven. Leave to cool in the pan, then slide a palette knife down each long side and remove using the parchment-paper handles. Cut into thick slices, and spread with dairy-free butter.

V/GF   PREP 5 mins / COOK 1 hr 15 mins

Crispy chocolate salted Thai rotis

Thai crispy roti would be my death-row dessert. It's crunchy on the outside and chewy on the inside, and made even more addictive with salted chocolate and a drizzle of condensed milk. Usually the roti dough is handmade and rested for hours before using, but here I've used phyllo sheets – a revelation – which makes them super quick to make.

NOTE Use the leftover condensed milk in iced coffee, or freeze for a future round of rotis. Milo, a malted chocolate powder, is available in major supermarkets.

MAKES 2 rotis, to serve 4

1 large egg

6 tbsp heavy (whipping) cream

¼ cup Milo, *plus extra to serve*

1 tbsp condensed milk, *plus extra to serve*

1 tsp flaky sea salt

6 sheets of phyllo pastry (each approx. 19 x 10 inches)

6 tbsp canola oil, *to shallow fry*

In a small bowl, whisk together the egg and 2 tablespoons of heavy cream until well mixed. In a separate bowl, mix together the Milo, condensed milk, salt and 4 tablespoons of heavy cream.

Lay the phyllo sheets in front of you, horizontally, on a large board or clean work surface and halve them down the middle. Place them on top of one another to one side, leaving lots of space to work with in front of you.

Take one single sheet and place it in front of you, then brush it with a thin layer of the egg cream, using a pastry brush. Take a second sheet and place it next to the brushed sheet. Brush it with the egg cream and then place the brushed side face down onto the existing brushed sheet. Repeat with the third, fourth and fifth sheet. When you come to the sixth, leave the top bare. You should have six sheets left.

Spoon half of the chocolate cream into the middle of the square and then bring each corner into the center point to create an envelope, making sure there is some overlap so that the roti can be sealed (and the chocolate cream won't leak out). It should be around 6 inches square, give or take.

Repeat this process to make a second roti using the remaining phyllo sheets and chocolate cream.

To cook the roti, take a nonstick frying pan. Place 4 tablespoons of oil in the pan over a medium heat. When it's very hot cook for 2 minutes on each side, or until dark brown spots form, pressing the square down as it cooks. Lever out with the spatula and place on a cutting board.

Add more oil to the pan if need be and cook the second roti, then place on the cutting board too. Put some Milo into a small sieve and tap to cover the pancakes, then drizzle over the condensed milk. Cut each roti into eight pieces and serve hot, straight from the cutting board.

PREP 2 mins / COOK 30 mins

Cereal milk ice-cream sandwiches

Christina Tosi of Momofuku introduced the world to cereal milk with a better understanding than most about how a particular flavor can take us back to a moment in time. Cornflakes, for instance, take me back to our wooden kitchen in Lincolnshire, circa 1990, Dad dipping toast in his chai ahead of a surreptitious wipe of his Tom Selleck–style moustache before whisking my sister and me, with our double plaits and rucksacks, into his Datsun 260Z for the school run.

NOTE Plastic wrap is the best option for lining the pan here but you can buy compostable. You'll need a blender to make this.

MAKES 12 ice-cream sandwiches

cornflake biscuit layers

5 cups cornflakes

5 tbsp superfine sugar

½ cup deodorized coconut oil, *melted*

8½ oz raspberries, *cut in half*

ice cream

2¼ cups cornflakes, *roughly bashed*

2 cups + 3 tbsp whole oat milk

1 cup roasted unsalted cashews

¼ cup superfine sugar

2 tbsp pure maple syrup

1 tsp pure vanilla extract

1 tbsp neutral oil, like canola or sunflower

salt

Line an 8- x 8-inch pan with plastic wrap, making sure there are no gaps and that it overhangs at the sides.

First, make the biscuit layers. Crush the cornflakes, either in a food processor or in the package – close the bag with a sandwich clip and use a rolling pin to crush the cornflakes into fine crumbs.

In a large bowl, combine the cornflake crumbs and sugar, then pour in the melted coconut oil and mix to combine. Tip two-thirds of the mixture into the lined pan (leave the other third in a bowl on the side for later) and press down as firmly as you can with the back of a spoon. Place the raspberry halves on top of the biscuit base, cut side down, in neat lines. Put the pan in the freezer while you make the ice cream.

To make the cereal milk, soak the bashed cornflakes in the oat milk for 20 minutes, until the milk turns oatmeal in color and the cornflakes are completely soggy.

Meanwhile, put the cashews into a small saucepan, pour over enough water to cover, bring to a boil, then simmer for 20 minutes. Drain, discarding the water, leave to cool, then tip into a blender. Sieve the milk from the cornflakes into a jug and use a spoon to squeeze out as much milk as possible, before discarding the soggy cornflakes.

Pour the cornflake milk into the blender with the drained cashews, add the sugar, maple syrup, vanilla extract, oil and a big pinch of salt, and blend on high speed for at least 4 minutes, until completely smooth.

Pour the ice-cream mix over the raspberries and freeze for 2 hours, or longer – until a finger is met with resistance. Remove from the freezer, sprinkle over the remaining cornflake crumbs and again use a spoon to press them down as firmly as you can. Freeze for another 2 or more hours, until completely solid.

Bring up to room temperature for 5 minutes before slicing into twelve bars and serving, or keep, sealed, in the freezer for up to three months.

V   PREP 5 mins / COOK 1 hr (plus 4 hrs to freeze)

Happy endings

A big bowl of chocolate mousse

I like big bowls and I cannot lie. I like to fill them to the brim with dessert and put them in the center of the table for people to pass around and help themselves to. It's always more generous, in my opinion, than going around the table, asking who would like dessert and, if so, what size portion they would like (I'm never keen to publicly own up to quite how big a portion I'd like, so I don't see why others should either).

Although this mousse is made with silken tofu, it's not vegan. The tofu replaces the faffy bit of making a custard with eggs. Here the tofu becomes custard-like after a quick whipping but needs the richness of the heavy cream (where vegan cream doesn't work as well) to add the velvety texture back in.

NOTE You'll need an electric mixer.

SERVES 6–8

10 oz silken tofu, *drained*

3 tbsp extra virgin olive oil , *plus extra to serve*

1 tbsp vanilla bean paste

1¼ cups heavy (whipping) cream

⅓ cup superfine sugar

7 oz good-quality dark chocolate (70%), *finely chopped*

¼ tsp salt

flaky sea salt, *to sprinkle*

Put the tofu, oil and vanilla paste into a bowl and whip to a creamy, custard-like consistency using an electric mixer. You'll need to scrape down the sides once or twice so that it is lump-free. Leave to one side, and tap the whisk attachments to remove any mixture, so you can use them again.

In a clean bowl, beat the heavy cream for 3 to 4 minutes, until you get soft peaks, then leave to one side.

Pour ⅓ cup of water and the sugar into a small saucepan over a low heat, stir until the sugar has dissolved, then take off the heat. Add the chocolate chips and the salt, and stir until all the chocolate has melted and is shinier than the hair in a Revlon advert.

Using a spatula, spoon the chocolate into the tofu bowl and mix well, then fold in the cream, taking care not to deflate the mixture as you turn it over and over, until it looks uniformly chocolate brown. Place in the fridge for at least an hour, and just before serving, sprinkle judiciously with flaky sea salt. Pour some extra virgin olive oil into a small jug and set out a little bowl of sea salt for people to help themselves, if they wish.

Vegan baked vanilla cheesecake

This recipe marked the fifth anniversary of my vegan column for the *Guardian*, and you can slap me with a (rubber) chicken if you don't think it's one of the best I've written so far. All thanks to the advances in vegan dairy – which is now better than ever – and the help of one reader, chef Matthew Sogorski. He could see I was having issues with getting some ingredients to behave, and came to my rescue. As a result, this isn't just a vegan cheesecake; it's a celebration of how far we've come in the world of vegan food, and a sweet bite of optimism for how far we might still go.

NOTE You'll need to start this recipe the night before or the morning of serving. Not all vegan cream cheeses will work here; it's very important to use one that's made with both coconut and soy, like GoVeggie vegan cream cheese or Trader Joe's brand. You'll need an 8-inch springform cake pan and a food processor.

SERVES 8

- 3½ oz shelled walnuts
- 3½ oz shelled pistachios
- 2 tbsp unsalted vegan butter, *melted*
- 2 tbsp agave or brown rice syrup
- ⅛ tsp salt
- 1½ lbs vegan cream cheese *(see note above)*
- 3½ oz silken tofu, *drained*
- ⅔ cup vegan heavy (whipping) cream
- 1 cup superfine sugar
- 1 tsp ground vanilla beans or 1½ tsp pure vanilla extract
- 3 tbsp cornstarch
- 1 lemon, *zested*

Preheat the oven to 425°F. Cut out a 15-inch square of parchment paper, crumple into a ball, rinse with tap water, then unravel and shake off. Push it into an 8-inch springform cake pan, flattening it against the sides and pressing it down and over the top edge.

Put the nuts and melted butter into a food processor, add the syrup and salt, then pulse to a coarse crumb – don't work it for too long, otherwise it will turn into nut butter. Tip the nut mix into the pan, scraping out the food processor really well, and use the back of a tablespoon to press it evenly all over the base of the pan.

Put the vegan cream cheese, tofu, cream, sugar, vanilla, cornstarch and lemon zest into the food processor bowl and blitz until smooth. Pour this evenly over the nut base, then bake for 50 minutes, rotating the pan 180 degrees once halfway through. After this time, the cheesecake should have some blackened patches on top and a gentle wobble.

Remove, leave to cool to room temperature, then refrigerate for at least 5 hours, or overnight, until properly fridge cold. Slice and serve.

Happy endings

Bubble tea ice cream

Ever since I can remember, my pull-it-out-the-bag dessert has always been good vanilla ice cream and a series of bowls of various toppings (like chopped fruit, chocolate and sprinkles) for people to help themselves to. This dessert is a step up from that and is built around my favorite Taiwanese brown-sugar bubble tea. It still revolves around good store-bought ice cream but has a lot more class for only a touch more effort.

NOTE The syrup and boba can both be made within 5 minutes and hours in advance. Keep both out of the fridge until serving (the boba tend to harden in the fridge). Make sure you buy "instant/quick" boba; you can find them in East Asian supermarkets and online (p 310). You'll need a pestle and mortar or something heavy to bash the nuts with.

SERVES 4

3 strong black tea bags (I like Assam)
1 cup soft light brown sugar, plus an extra teaspoon
heaping ¼ cup salted peanuts
¾ cup instant boba balls
2 cups good vanilla ice cream, vegan or dairy

To make the tea syrup, place ⅔ cup of water in a small saucepan over a medium heat and bring it to a boil. Turn the heat off and steep the tea bags for 4 minutes, then squeeze them gently but firmly to extract as much liquid as possible as you take them out. Add the sugar to the tea and stir to dissolve, then bring the mixture to a boil again over a medium heat for 3 to 4 minutes, or until the sugar starts to form big glossy bubbles and crawl up the pan. Turn the heat off and leave to cool completely.

Using a pestle and mortar, or a small blender, grind the peanuts and a teaspoon of sugar to a fine powder and leave to one side.

Cook the boba according to the package instructions. Drain in a sieve and rinse under the cold tap until they're cool, then drain very well again and place in a food container. Spoon over 2 tablespoons of the cooled syrup, close the container and leave out on the counter until ready to serve.

To serve, place a scoop (or two) of ice cream in each bowl. Spoon a tablespoon of tea syrup, or enough to cover the ice cream, over each portion. Sprinkle over a tablespoon of ground peanuts and finally, using a slotted spoon, put a quarter of the boba around the ice cream in each bowl.

Happy endings

Matai's coconut and cardamom dream cake

Coconut and cardamom is a very Indian flavor combination, but this cake is Danish. I first ate it embedded in an ice cream made by Matai Jowitt at his fantastic ice-cream shop, Creamo's, in Ashburton, Devon. After badgering him for the recipe, he sent me a hand-typed list of ingredients and some, but not all, the instructions, as a cook's challenge, which resulted in this beautiful cake. The best bit by far is the thick, crunchy and chewy coconut caramel topping, which forms in the oven and cracks away to reveal a yielding soft sponge.

NOTE You'll need an 8½-inch cake pan and an electric whisk for this recipe.

SERVES 10–12

cake
5 tbsp unsalted butter, *plus extra to grease the pan*
⅔ cup whole milk
1 tsp vanilla bean paste
1 lime, *zested*
3 large eggs
1 cup + 2 tbsp superfine sugar
1½ cups all-purpose flour
2 tsp baking powder
¾ tsp ground cardamom
½ tsp salt

coconut topping
½ cup unsalted butter
⅓ cup whole milk
1¼ cups soft light brown sugar
1 tsp ground cardamom
1¾ cups unsweetened shredded coconut

to serve
1¼ cups heavy (whipping) cream
1 tsp vanilla bean paste
1 lime

Preheat the oven to 400°F. Cut a circle of parchment paper big enough to line the base of a 8½-inch cake pan, and another long strip to go all around the inside, making sure that it will come 1 inch above the top of the pan. Grease the pan, line with the parchment paper and set aside.

Melt the butter for the cake in a small saucepan, leave it to cool for 3 minutes, then add the milk, vanilla bean paste and the lime zest. Mix and leave to one side. Put the eggs and sugar into a mixing bowl and mix with the electric whisk until pale, creamy and thick. The mixture should be at ribbon stage (thick enough to hold its shape when drizzled back on itself). Sift the flour, baking powder, cardamom and salt into a large bowl. Mix well, then fold in the eggs and sugar, then the milk and butter mixture, until well combined. Pour the batter into the pan and bake for 30 minutes.

As soon as the cake hits the oven, make the coconut topping. Put all the topping ingredients except the shredded coconut into a small saucepan, bring it to a boil, and boil for 1 minute, then take off the heat. Five minutes before the cake comes out, reheat the pan until the topping is thin and runny, then take off the heat and add the shredded coconut.

When the cake's time is up, remove it (but leave the oven on) – it will be wobbly and starting to turn golden on top. Gently and evenly layer the coconut mixture over the cake, making sure not to press down, then return to the oven and bake for another 25 minutes. Take out of the oven and leave the cake to cool completely in the pan before removing and decorating.

Just before serving, put the cream and vanilla bean paste into a bowl. Using the electric whisk, beat the cream to soft peaks. Top the cake with the cream, then grate over the zest.

1000-hole pancakes with peanuts and chocolate

After multiple decades on Earth, I thought I knew all there was to know about pancakes – until I met *martabak manis* at a hawker market in Singapore. It's what I imagine crumpet-lovers dream about: a giant, sweet, crunchy, soft pancake with a thousand deep holes ready to be saturated with butter and, in this case, chocolate and salted peanuts. It was a revelation to me, and has since been a serious challenger to the incumbent weekend pancake recipe in the Sodha household.

NOTE This is a yeasted recipe, so you'll need to factor in an hour for the mixture to proof.

MAKES 2 large pancakes, to serve 4

batter
1¼ cups whole oat milk
1⅔ cups all-purpose flour
½ tsp salt
1 tsp quick-rise yeast
4 tsp apple cider vinegar
½ tsp baking soda
canola oil, *for frying*

filling
2 tbsp superfine sugar
2 tbsp vegan butter
1 square (½ oz) of vegan dark
  chocolate, *grated*
a large handful of salted peanuts,
  finely chopped

If the oat milk has been in the fridge, warm it to body temperature, either in the microwave or a small saucepan.

In a large bowl, combine the flour, salt, yeast and oat milk, and beat well with a spoon – you want to develop some gluten here, so beat for a couple of minutes, then set aside for an hour, so the yeast has time to get active and the mix has roughly doubled in size.

After the hour is up, combine the vinegar and baking soda in a small bowl and stir this into the batter mix.

Put ½ teaspoon of oil into a good nonstick pancake or frying pan for which you have a lid, set it over a medium heat and swirl to distribute the oil over the surface of the pan.

When hot, add half the batter to the pan, using a wooden spoon to help it into an even layer. Leave to cook for 5 minutes, keeping an eye on the bottom to make sure it's not darkening too quickly. If it is, turn the heat down. You should see hundreds of little bubbles appearing across the surface. When the holes are distinct and open, scatter half the sugar over the top of the pancake and cover the pan with the lid.

After a minute, once the sugar has melted, remove the pancake from the pan and, while it's still hot, spread with half the butter. Scatter over half the chocolate, followed by half the chopped peanuts. Repeat with the remaining batter and toppings. To serve in the traditional manner fold the pancakes in half, cut into quarters and eat. Or else, slice and gobble it up as it is.

V PREP 10 mins / COOK 10 mins (plus 1 hr to proof)

Thai mango sticky rice

My relationship with mangoes can be split into two halves: before I first ate Thai mango sticky rice and after. Before, I thought of myself as a mango purist and that nothing could beat an Alphonso fresh out of the box. But I was wrong. There is something extraordinarily special about the marriage between milky, sweet coconut and delightfully chewy, sticky rice that brings out the best and sunniest side of any mango. Eating it is pure joy, so make it while you can (i.e., while mango season lasts: from April to July).

NOTE An inexpensive bamboo steamer is key here. You'll also need a thin, clean kitchen towel or muslin to steam the rice, and to set aside 30 minutes to soak the rice before cooking.

SERVES 4

1 cup glutinous or Thai sticky rice
1 x 14-oz can of organic whole coconut milk
2 tbsp superfine sugar
¼ tsp salt
4 Alphonso, honey or Kesar mangoes
1 lime, *quartered*

Place the rice in a large bowl and cover with water. Agitate the rice with your hand until the water turns cloudy, then drain and repeat, until the water runs clear. Drain again, then place in your large bowl, cover with hand-hot water and leave to soak for half an hour. Pop the can of coconut milk in the freezer until needed.

After the soaking time, drain the rice. Line the top layer of your bamboo steamer with the kitchen towel and place the rice inside. Using your fingertips, even it out to a thin layer. Wrap the sides of the kitchen towel over the top of the rice and close the top of the steamer.

Fill a frying pan, large enough to fit the steamer in, with 1 inch of water and place on the heat. Bring the water to a boil, then reduce the heat to a simmer and carefully lower the steamer into the water. Cook for 20 to 25 minutes, or until the rice is tender, topping up the water in the pan if need be.

While the rice is cooking, make the coconut cream. Remove the coconut milk from the freezer and (without shaking the can) scrape ¾ cup + 5 tsp of thick cream into a small saucepan. If there isn't enough, top it up with coconut water to make up ¾ cup + 5 tsp (keep the rest of the water for smoothies), then add the sugar and salt. Stir to mix and bring to a boil, then take off the heat.

Next, peel the mangoes and cut off the four "cheeks" from each one (keep the stones to nibble on), then thinly slice each cheek.

When the rice has steamed, carefully unwrap the kitchen towel, taking care as the steam will be very hot. Tip the rice into a bowl and pour over most of the coconut cream, reserving ¼ cup for serving. Mix using a fork, then cover and put to one side, so the rice can absorb the cream.

To serve, put the rice into four bowls in neat mounds. Spread mango slices over each portion of rice, squeeze a little lime juice on top, then pour a tablespoon of reserved coconut cream over each one.

V/GF   PREP 5 mins / COOK 40 mins (plus 30 mins to soak)

Matcha mochi cakes with sesame seed brittle

Butter mochi cakes, like this one, hail from Hawaii. While the Japanese and Chinese have similar chewy desserts, no one else, as far as I can see, uses the unique combination of melted butter and coconut milk in their recipes. Usually, the cake is baked in a single pan, which yields dense, sticky and chewy squares. I prefer baking them in muffin pans. It gives each small cake a glorious surround-sound golden crust, as well as the typical mochi center, and so in my eyes you get the best of both worlds.

NOTE You'll need to buy glutinous rice flour for this recipe – available in East Asian supermarkets and online (p 310). You'll also need a 12-cup muffin pan.

MAKES 12

cakes

¼ cup unsalted butter, *plus extra for greasing the tin*

1⅔ cups glutinous rice flour

1 tsp baking powder

½ tsp salt

1½ tbsp matcha powder

1 cup superfine sugar

2 large eggs

2 tsp vanilla bean paste

1 x 14-oz can of coconut milk

to decorate

¾ oz raw sesame seeds *(I use white and black, mixed)*

1 tbsp superfine sugar

a pinch of salt

3½ oz white chocolate, *finely chopped*

Preheat the oven to 400°F. Using a pastry brush, grease the inside and just around the outside of the 12-cup muffin pan with soft butter.

Put the flour, baking powder, salt and matcha powder into a large mixing bowl and whisk to mix. Melt the butter in a heatproof bowl in 10-second bursts in the microwave. Leave to cool for a few minutes, then transfer to another large mixing bowl, along with the sugar and eggs. Whisk by hand for around 3 minutes, until pale, then add the vanilla bean paste and coconut milk and whisk again. Pour the wet mixture into the dry and whisk well until smooth. Spoon the batter evenly into the pan. Gently shake the pan to level the batter and remove any air bubbles.

Bake for 30 minutes, then rotate the pan and bake for a further 20 minutes. Test with a skewer: it should come out clean; if not, bake for a further 5 minutes. When the pan has cooled enough to handle, remove the cakes. Slide a palette knife around the edges of each cake and carefully release. Place on a wire rack to cool.

To make the sesame seed brittle, place the sesame seeds in a small non-stick frying pan along with the sugar, a tablespoon of water and a pinch of salt. Put the pan over a low to medium heat and stir: the water will evaporate and the seeds will form a clump. Keep stirring for around 6 minutes, until the seeds start to dry out and separate a little, then tip out onto a plate and leave to cool.

Once the cakes have cooled, put the white chocolate in a heatproof bowl and melt in 20-second bursts in the microwave, stirring each time until almost all the pieces are melted (the rest will melt in the residual heat). Place the cooled cakes on a tray or parchment paper and drizzle over the chocolate using a spoon. Then break the brittle into even pieces and put a couple on each cake. Leave the chocolate to set. The cakes are at their best when eaten fresh, but will keep well in an airtight container for up to three days.

Pictured overleaf

Happy endings

Extra helpings / helpful extras

Here you'll find all the supporting acts you'll need to give your dinner the razzle-dazzle it deserves. Some of these recipes have been selected from my archive to help you complete your meal.

Rice

To boil or to steam? Either way, make sure you get the rice going before cooking the main event. Rice retains its heat in a lidded pan for up to an hour and can easily be microwaved if cold. Pop it into a heatproof container, add a splash of water, cover with a plate and heat in 30-second bursts, stirring, until piping hot.

Now back to the debate: I prefer to steam my rice because it absorbs the exact amount of water needed and retains any flavor you might want it to absorb. But there's no judgement here if you're a boiler.

Jasmine rice

This is a great everyday rice as it does not need soaking. You can just rinse it in a sieve under the cold tap until the water runs clear, drain, then throw it straight into a pan, making it perfect for weeknight suppers.

Servings	Rice	Water to steam
For 2	¾ cup	1¼ cups freshly boiled
For 4	1½ cups	1¾ cups freshly boiled

To prep: Place the rice in a sieve and wash thoroughly, agitating it with your hand, until the water runs clear.

To steam: Place the drained rice in a pan for which you have a tight-fitting lid, with the freshly boiled water (see above for quantities). Bring to a boil, put the lid on, then turn the heat down to a whisper. Cook for 15 minutes, then take off the heat and leave to steam with the lid on for a further 5 to 10 minutes.

To boil: Place the drained rice in a pan and cover with plenty of freshly boiled water. Bring back up to a boil, simmer for 15 minutes, or until tender, then drain.

Basmati rice

I love basmati's elegant, long and slender grains, which will always smell and taste of home to me. It needs only a little more attention than jasmine.

Servings	Rice	Water to steam
For 2	¾ cup	1¼ cups freshly boiled
For 4	1½ cups	1¾ cups freshly boiled

Prep: Place the basmati in a bowl, cover with water and agitate with your hands until the water turns cloudy. Drain and repeat until the water is clear (this will get rid of the excess starch and give you fluffy basmati), then soak the rice for 10 minutes in hand-hot water, or 20 minutes in cold water, and drain again.

To steam: Place the drained rice in a saucepan for which you have a tight-fitting lid, along with the freshly boiled water (see above for quantities). Bring to a boil, put the lid on, then turn the heat down to a whisper. Cook for 10 minutes, then take off the heat and leave to steam with the lid on for a further 10 minutes.

To boil: Place the drained rice in a large pan and cover with plenty of freshly boiled water. Bring back up to a boil, simmer for 10 to 12 minutes, or until tender, then drain. Cover with a clean kitchen towel and leave to rest for 5 to 10 minutes.

Short-grain or sushi rice

This rice is popular across Korea, Thailand and Japan. These short, stubby grains have a delightfully chewy texture. Due to the starch present in the grains, they cling on to one another, making them great to eat with chopsticks. I like to serve this rice using the upside-down bowl trick to mold a small mound, topped with fried tofu or sambal, or indented with the back of a spoon to house a soy-cured egg yolk.

Servings	Rice	Water to steam
For 2	¾ cup	¾ cup at room temperature
For 4	1½ cups	1⅔ cups at room temperature

Prep: Place the rice in a medium-sized pan for which you have a tight-fitting lid and cover with lukewarm water. Agitate with your hand until the water turns cloudy, then drain and repeat, until the water runs clear. Cover with warm water and leave to soak for 5 minutes, then drain again.

To cook: Place the drained rice back in the pan with the right quantity of water (see above for quantities). Put the lid on, bring to a boil, then turn the heat down to a whisper and cook for 10 minutes. Take off the heat and leave to steam with the lid on for a further 10 minutes.

Breads

Making your own bread is always going to be more therapeutic and delicious than buying it, but in holding the torch for an easy dinner, I should tell you that many supermarkets, especially Indian and South East Asian, sell a great variety of ready-made breads. Look for chapattis in the supermarket bread aisle, and frozen paratha, aloo paratha and bao in Asian supermarkets. Usually, you can freeze them and either microwave or pan-fry them as needed. Wrap in foil and a clean kitchen towel to keep warm.

For other breads in the book, see the quick paratha on p 190, the tattie rotis on p 188 and the crispy chocolate salted Thai rotis on p 286.

Ben's flatbreads V

These quick and beautifully soft flatbreads are Ben Benton's (of Ben Benton strikes again fame, on p 36). If you're not going to use all the dough in one go, roll them out after proofing, layer between parchment paper and freeze in a food-storage container. They can be cooked from frozen.

MAKES 8 flatbreads

1 x ¼-oz package of instant dry yeast
1 cup + 4 tsp hand-hot water
3¾ cups white bread flour, plus extra to dust
1 tsp salt

Put the yeast into a small bowl or jug, add about 1½ tablespoons of the warm water and mix to a smooth liquid. In a large bowl, mix the flour and salt, then add the yeast mixture and the remaining water. Use your hands or a metal spoon to mix until all the liquid is incorporated but the mixture is still lumpy, then set it aside for 10 minutes.

After this time, knead the dough for 5 minutes, or until smooth and springy, then shape into eight balls, around 3 oz each. Place on a tray or work surface, cover with a clean kitchen towel and allow to proof for 5 minutes.

You can either cook your flatbreads in the oven or use a heavy-based or cast-iron pan. If you're cooking your flatbreads in the oven, preheat the oven to its highest setting, move two racks to the top of the oven and line two baking sheets with lightly oiled aluminum foil. While the oven is heating up, roll the dough balls into flatbreads about 6 inches in diameter, dusting the surface with a little flour in between them to stop them sticking. Place two flatbreads on each baking sheet, side by side, and bake for 3 to 5 minutes, until there is no uncooked dough.

If using a pan, put it over a medium heat until it's very hot, then pan-fry the flatbreads for 3 to 5 minutes, turning them halfway through the cooking time.

Elephant ear garlic naan

This is based on Harsha Aunty's naan recipe, which I adapted for *Fresh India* to include the garlic butter. It has 2,097 five-star ratings on the *New York Times* website. Go, Harsha Aunty!

MAKES 4 big sharing naans, for 6 to 8 people

3¾ cups white bread flour, plus extra to dust
canola oil
¼ cup plain full-fat yogurt
1 x ¼-oz package of instant dry yeast
2 tsp superfine sugar
salt
1 tsp baking powder
1 cup + 5 tsp whole milk, hand hot
½ cup unsalted butter
4 cloves of garlic, crushed
1 tsp nigella seeds, to sprinkle

Place the flour in a large bowl. Make a well and add 2 tablespoons of oil, the yogurt, yeast, sugar, 2 teaspoons of salt and the baking powder. Mix through with your fingers until the ingredients resemble breadcrumbs, then mix in the warm milk.

Knead the mixture on a clean and well-floured surface. It will be very sticky at first, soft but fairly robust. Knead for around 5 minutes and shape into a ball, then scrape any dough off your hands using a spoon (the best way, I've found) and settle the dough by rubbing a teaspoon of oil all over it.

Transfer the dough to a bowl in which it can double in size, cover it with a clean kitchen towel or plastic wrap and leave it in a warm place for at least an hour. (Mum leaves hers in the airing cupboard; I leave mine in an oven that has been heated to 230°F for 10 minutes, then switched off.)

To make the garlic butter, put the butter into a small saucepan over a low to medium heat and, when melted, add the garlic and a couple of big pinches of salt. Cook for 5 minutes, then take off the heat and leave to one side.

When the dough has risen, preheat the oven to 475°F and separate the dough into four pieces. Put three pieces back into the bowl and cover while you roll and cook the first. Roll the dough into a ball and flatten it between your palms. Use a rolling pin to roll out into a triangular elephant-ear shape around 10 inches long. Add a little oil while you're rolling if need be.

In the meantime, put a thin, lightly oiled baking sheet into the oven for 5 minutes. When hot, lay the naan on the baking sheet and sprinkle with nigella seeds. Cook for 5 minutes on the top shelf, then remove. The naan should be soft, fluffy and cooked through, with no doughy spots. Brush or drizzle on the garlic butter and repeat with the other naans. Keep them warm by creating a foil nest for them and try not to eat them before serving.

Mum's chapattis   V

NOTE: If you don't need as many as twelve chapattis, feel free to make half or three-quarters of the recipe. I usually make two per person.

MAKES 12, to serve 4 to 6

3½ cups chapatti flour, or 1¾ cups whole-grain and 1¾ cups all-purpose flour, *plus extra to dust*
canola oil
½ tsp salt
1¼ cups water, *hand hot*

Put the flour into a bowl, add the salt and mix together. Make a well in the middle, add 3 tablespoons of oil and combine, using your fingers, until the mixture resembles fine breadcrumbs. Pour in 1 cup of the water, then add the rest little by little – you may not need it all – until you can knead the mixture into a soft and pliable dough, which will take up to 8 minutes.

Lightly rub the dough with a teaspoon of oil (so it doesn't dry out) and put it to one side. Dust a work surface with flour and keep a bowl of flour in which to dip the balls of dough, a spatula (or chapatti press) and a plate for your cooked chapattis to one side. Once all is ready, divide your dough into sixteen pieces. Put a nonstick frying pan on a medium to high heat.

Take one piece of dough, roll it into a ball between your palms, coat it generously with flour, flatten it into a disk and then roll it out to around 4 inches in diameter. Lightly coat both sides in flour again, then roll out to around 6 inches and put it face side down on the hot pan.

Wait for the edges to color white and for the chapatti to start to bubble (30 to 40 seconds), then turn it over and cook it for the same amount of time. Turn it over again – it should start to puff up at this point, so press it down gently with the flat side of the spatula – and cook for about 10 seconds, then turn it over again and do the same.

Check that all the dough is cooked (any uncooked spots will look dark and doughy) and put on a plate. Cover with a kitchen towel or wrap in foil to keep warm, then repeat with the rest of the dough.

Many Indian women have mastered the art of rolling out a new chapatti in exactly the time it takes to cook one, keeping a close eye on both the cooking and the rolling. It is enormously efficient and rewarding, but many burnt chapattis have been sacrificed in getting there, so don't worry if it takes a while.

Pickles, chutneys and other bits

There are a number of pickles and dips scattered throughout the book – for example, lime pickle yogurt (p 140), pickled onions (p 181), pickled turnip (p 50) and soy pickled cucumbers (p 271), but here are some others I couldn't live without.

Quick frying-pan lemon pickle

V/GF

SERVES 4

2 lemons
canola oil
½ tsp black mustard seeds
1 clove of garlic, *thinly sliced*
1 red chilli, *finely chopped*
salt

Top and tail one lemon, cut it into four, then cut each quarter into very thin slices (use your sharpest knife), removing any pips. Put the slices in a bowl, and juice the other lemon over the top.

On a very low flame, heat 2 tablespoons of oil in a pan for which you have a lid. Add the mustard seeds and garlic, and when the garlic turns pale gold, add the chilli, lemon slices, lemon juice and ½ teaspoon of salt. Stir to mix, cover, and leave to cook for 5 minutes. Remove the lid, cook for 5 minutes more, until the oil starts to split from the lemons, then take off the heat and leave to cool. This pickle can be kept in a sealed container or jar in the fridge for a up to a week.

Sodha family cilantro chutney

V/GF

MAKES a small jar

3½ oz fresh cilantro, *thick stems removed*
scant ½ cup salted peanuts
2 green finger (or serrano) chillies, *chopped*
4 tsp soft light brown sugar
¼ cup lemon juice, *from 2 lemons*
2 tbsp canola oil
1 tsp salt

Wash the cilantro leaves (even if they're from a package, it's still useful to wash them as they will blend more easily) and roughly chop. Put them into a blender and add the rest of the ingredients and 2 tablespoons of water. Blend, scrape down, and add another tablespoon of water if need be. Taste and check it's as salty, sweet and hot as you like it. This chutney can be kept in small tub or jar in the fridge for up to a week.

Fresh hot chilli chutney

V/GF

This chutney adds a bright, fresh, zingy heat to whatever it touches. It is best eaten straight away, but it can be kept in the fridge in a sealed container or jar for a few days.

SERVES 4 (makes a small jar)

4 mild red chillies (2 oz), *chopped*
1 x 1 inch ginger, *chopped*
3 cloves of garlic, *chopped*
½ tsp salt
1½ tsp superfine sugar
2 tsp toasted sesame oil
1½ tbsp lime juice, *from 1 lime*
2 tsp rice vinegar

Pop all the ingredients in a blender, ideally a small one like a Nutribullet, and blend to a smooth sauce.

Cucumber and mint raita
VO/GF

An excellent side to any Indian curry or subji, but highly recommended as an accompaniment to fresh hot flatbreads (pp 305–6) as eaten in the Turkish manner.

SERVES 4 (makes a small bowlful)

½ tsp cumin seeds
1 English cucumber (8½ oz)
1 cup plain Greek or dairy-free yogurt
½ tsp salt
½ oz fresh mint, *leaves picked and finely chopped*

Put the cumin seeds into a cold frying pan over a low heat and fry for 3½ minutes, tossing every 30 seconds or so, until they're darker and fragrant. Grind to a coarse dust using a pestle and mortar.

Grate the cucumber into a bowl, add ¼ teaspoon of salt, leave to stand in a sieve over a bowl for 5 minutes, then squeeze out and discard all the water. Put the yogurt into a serving bowl, add the cucumber, mint leaves, a big pinch of the toasted cumin and the final ¼ teaspoon of salt. Stir to mix, then sprinkle some more cumin over the top.

Sesame dipping sauce
V

A good thing to dip cooked greens into (or pour over), but especially broccolini.

SERVES 4

¼ cup tahini
1 tbsp toasted sesame oil
1½ tbsp light soy sauce
1 tbsp agave or brown rice syrup
½ x ½ inch ginger, *grated*

Place all the ingredients in a bowl and mix together, then add a little water to help loosen it up to dip consistency.

Sweet soy sauce
V

A good sub for kecap manis.

2 tbsp dark soy sauce
2 tbsp light agave syrup

Mix together in a small bowl and double or triple to your heart's content.

Soy-cured egg yolk
DF

I love to eat this mixed into sesame rice (p 240). I serve the rice hot, in an upturned mound, and make a dent in the middle in which the yolk can sit. Serve with extra soy sauce and vegan fish sauce on the side.

SERVES 1–2

3½ tbsp light soy sauce
3½ tbsp mirin
2 egg yolks

Pour the soy sauce and mirin into a small bowl, stir, then gently lower in the egg yolks. Leave to marinate for 20 minutes, then carefully spoon each yolk out of the soy mixture and onto some rice.

Pea and wasabi dip
GF

MAKES a small bowlful

1¾ cups frozen baby peas
3 oz full-fat cream cheese
2 tbsp canola oil
2½ tsp (½ oz) wasabi paste
up to ¼ tsp salt

Put the frozen peas into a bowl and pour over enough freshly boiled water from the kettle to cover. Leave for 2 minutes, then drain and place in a blender with the cream cheese, oil and wasabi paste. Blend until smooth, then taste and add a little salt or more wasabi if you wish, blend again, then serve.

ONLINE SUPPLIERS

General

For East and South East Asian ingredients

99 Ranch is a nationwide pan-Asian grocery store chain. www.99ranch.com

For South Asian ingredients

Kalustyan's is a New York–based grocery store that ships nationwide and stocks everything from date syrup and rosewater to moong dal and dried fenugreek. www.foodsofnations.com

Specialists

Korean specialists

Get your kimchi, gochujang and K-pop from one store: www.hmart.com

Indian specialists

For curry leaves, Indian red chile powder and all the dal your heart could desire, visit www.ishopindian.com

Thai specialists

For galangal, Thai basil and Makrut lime leaves: www.grocerythai.com

For spices

This store stocks single-origin spices with a more transparent supply chain than what you buy in the supermarket. www.oaktownspiceshop.com

For flours and vegan baking ingredients

Ingredients like fine semolina, almond flour and ground flaxseeds are all available from Bob's Red Mill. www.bobsredmill.com

Thanks

It takes many hands and a lot of hard work to make a cookbook, and I would love to thank those who dedicated their time, effort and care to making this one.

Thanks to my family:

To Hugh, for being everything: my copilot in love, life and parenting; my biggest champion and well-worn shoulder. Thanks especially for caretaking the girls while I was cooking, writing or researching, for the (endless) chats about the book and for dealing with the disruption of my writing it with such grace.

To Arya and Yogi, for all the magic, but in particular for the mini hot snacks, double jumps of joy, huggles and "true love" kisses.

To Meron, my Ethiopian sister, for your incredible support and for looking after all of us; and to Mum, Dad, Peter, Roubina, Barbara and Kevin for all your kind help.

Thanks to my team:

To Hannah C. M. – a hat tip for being the absolute best recipe tester and assistant. Thanks for caring about each and every recipe as much as I do and for always fighting the corner of the home cook. Thanks also for the very happy decade-long friendship that now stretches from the English Sea to the Indian Ocean – and for sticking with me after the big move. Props to Conor, Oisin and Marlow for being hungry enthusiasts. To my other recipe testers, Anna Ansari and Nicola Roberts, who have come along on this particular journey and smashed it, enormous thanks also.

To Ben Benton, for the good times but in particular for the inspiration and help with developing new recipes. You're an obscenely talented cook and writer and I'm incredibly thankful for the help you've given me over the years. To Anais Ca Dao, for being an excellent trip researcher, eater and companion in Thailand, Taiwan and Vietnam. Thanks for teaching me new flavors and techniques and for the laughs, the slot-machine animals and being incomparably you.

To Kali Jago, Matai Jowitt, Anshu Ahuja and Mitra Nataraj, for working on or contributing recipes; to Ben Adamo, for inspiration; and to Chris Evans, for your thoughts on pizza making at home and bread knives.

Thanks to the Penguins:

I'll be forever grateful to my previous editor, Juliet Annan, who I worked with on my first three books. Thanks for your many years of service and your belief in me, and for commissioning this book.

To my current editor, Helen Garnons-Williams, for being so supportive (tolerant), encouraging and open-minded throughout the process. It's been a joy to work with you. Thanks also to the wider team, Richard Bravery, Saffron Stocker, Jon Gray, Chris Bentham, Gail Jones, Ella Harold, Rosie Furlong, Annie Moore, Annie Lucas, Samantha Fanaken, Emma Brown and Jane Gentle, for being fun to work with but also for being extraordinarily talented and collaborative.

To Annie Underwood, for going the extra mile to get the book printed and distributed. And to Caroline Pretty, my copyeditor, for going through the manuscript with a fine-tooth comb and making it fit for use for cooks up and down the country.

Thanks to the Flatiron team:

To Will Schwalbe and Julie Will, my excellent American editors, thank you for believing in my work, for publishing me in North America and for being hugely enjoyable to work with.

To Tracy Bordian, thank you for all your diligent and patient work in Americanizing the book. Many thanks also to Sydney Jeon for editorial assistance, Maris Tasaka and Nancy Trypuc for all things marketing, Joanne Raymond for publicity and Emily Walters for production.

Finally, many thanks to Megan Lynch for having me on board at Flatiron. I couldn't wish for a better transatlantic home.

Thanks to the book shoot team:

To David Loftus, for the forever beauty – for capturing my food in a way that looks sometimes (and embarrassingly) better than in real life, and for your calm, intuitive style. Your love for what you do shines brightly from every page.

To Emily Ezekiel, the wonder of wonders. What a natural talent, what an eye for color, what grace under pressure and what a jewelry collection! Thanks to you and your hard-working team: Jodene Jordan, Joseph Dennison Carey, Poppy Bertram, Lu Cottle and Sophie. And a special thank-you to Alex Cunningham and Jo Clayton for helping me with the family shoot.

To Poppy Royds and the team at Natoora, for providing me and the shoot team with some of the finest vegetables and ingredients available in the UK.

Thanks to the guardians:

To Tim Lusher and Bob Granleese, for having me on board and for your continued support and understanding during my time off to have babies and work on the book. And thanks for all the editing, Bob.

Thanks to my agent:

Agent Jane Finigan! I'm exceptionally lucky to know you and I am so very proud to work with you. Thank you for being the best agent a writer could have.

Thanks to my supporters:

To Julie Beckett and Alexandra Knowles, for giving me new eyes with which to see the world – I don't know of a greater gift. To my friends who have encouraged me from the sidelines (and the school gates) but especially Matt Maude, Anouk van den Eijnde, Chris Chapman, Sonal Sodha and little Dick Whittington.

And finally, to all the home cooks. A huge thanks for all your kind messages, photos and emails over the years. Seeing photos of your well-used books makes me feel like I'm in the right place at the right time, doing the right thing – which continues to be a very wonderful experience.

Index

Page references in *italics* indicate images.

To my favorite dinner-table companions, Hugh, Arya and Yogi;
and to two extraordinary women in my life, Hannah and Meron

www.flatironbooks.com

Photography copyright © David Loftus, 2024
Illustrations copyright © Jonathan Gray / gray318, 2024

Library of Congress Cataloging-in-Publication Data

Names: Sodha, Meera, author.
Title: Dinner : 120 vegan and vegetarian recipes for the most important meal of the day / Meera Sodha.
Description: First U.S. edition. | New York, NY : Flatiron Books, 2025. | Includes index.
Identifiers: LCCN 2024038905 | ISBN 9781250358158 (paper over board) | ISBN 9781250358165 (ebook)
Subjects: LCSH: Vegan cooking. | Dinners and dining. | LCGFT: Cookbooks.
Classification: LCC TX837 .S679 2025 | DDC 641.5/6362—dc23/eng/20240910
LC record available at https://lccn.loc.gov/2024038905

Our books may be purchased in bulk for promotional, educational, or business
use. Please contact your local bookseller or the Macmillan Corporate and
Premium Sales Department at 1-800-221-7945, extension 5442, or by email at
MacmillanSpecialMarkets@macmillan.com.

Originally published in Great Britain by Fig Tree, an imprint of Penguin Random House, UK

First U.S. Edition: 2025

10 9 8 7 6 5 4 3 2 1